Exercises in Sorting and Searching

for OCR GCSE Computer Science J277

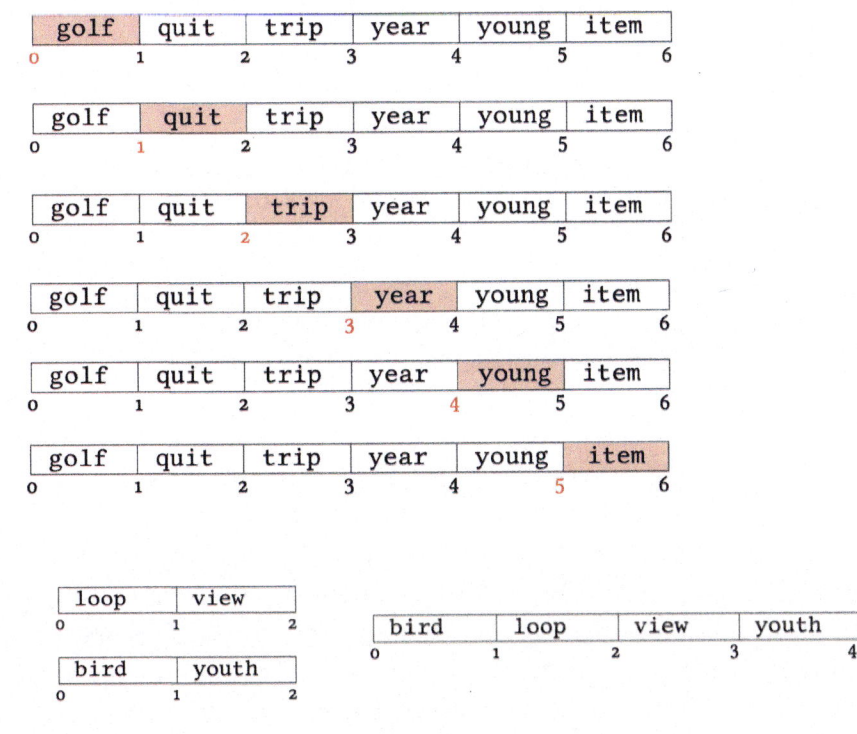

Alfred M. Capone

Contents

Contents — 2

I Sorting algorithms — 7

1 Insertion sort — 9
- 1.1 Worked Example 1: Sorting a four element array 9
- 1.2 Worked Example 2: Sorting a four element array 12
- 1.3 Worked Example 3: Sorting a six element array 14
- 1.4 Worked Example 4: Sorting a five element array 18
- 1.5 Worked Example 5: Sorting a seven element array 21
- 1.6 Worked Example 6: Sorting a five element array 26
- 1.7 Worked Example 7: Sorting a four element array 29
- 1.8 Worked Example 8: Sorting a seven element array 31

2 Bubble sort — 37
- 2.1 Worked Example 1: Sorting a five element array (in three passes) 37
- 2.2 Worked Example 2: Sorting an seven element array (in six passes) 40
- 2.3 Worked Example 3: Sorting a five element array (in five passes) 46
- 2.4 Worked Example 4: Sorting a six element array (in five passes) 50
- 2.5 Worked Example 5: Sorting a six element array (in five passes) 54
- 2.6 Worked Example 6: Sorting a five element array (in four passes) 58
- 2.7 Worked Example 7: Sorting a five element array (in three passes) 61
- 2.8 Worked Example 8: Sorting a seven element array (in five passes) 64

3 Mergesort — 69
- 3.1 Worked Example 1: Sorting a four element array 69
- 3.2 Worked Example 2: Sorting a four element array 72
- 3.3 Worked Example 3: Sorting a six element array 75
- 3.4 Worked Example 4: Sorting an array with six elements 79
- 3.5 Worked Example 5: Sorting an array with six elements 83
- 3.6 Worked Example 6: Sorting an array with five elements 87

Exercises in Sorting and Searching

 3.7 Worked Example 7: Sorting an array with four elements 91
 3.8 Worked Example 8: Sorting an array with four elements 94

II Searching algorithms   97

4 Linear search   99
 4.1 Worked Example 1: Present in middle of input array 99
 4.2 Worked Example 2: Not present in input array 100
 4.3 Worked Example 3: Present at end of array 102
 4.4 Worked Example 4: Not present in input array 104
 4.5 Worked Example 5: Present at start of array 106
 4.6 Worked Example 6: Not present in input array 107
 4.7 Worked Example 7: Present at start of array 109
 4.8 Worked Example 8: Not present in input array 110

5 Binary search   111
 5.1 Worked Example 1: Finding an item near the end of the input array 111
 5.2 Worked Example 2: Searching for an query not present in the input array 113
 5.3 Worked Example 3: Searching for an element near the start of the input array . . . 115
 5.4 Worked Example 4: Searching for an element not present in the input array 117
 5.5 Worked Example 5: Searching for an element not present in the input array 118
 5.6 Worked Example 6: Searching for a element not present in the input array 119
 5.7 Worked Example 7: Getting lucky on the first guess 121
 5.8 Worked Example 8: Searching for a element not present in the input array 122

What you'll get from this book

I wrote this book because I'm fed up with seeing my students lose marks on exam questions which ask them to run search algorithms and sorting algorithms and, more generally, struggling with stepping through algorithms and not having suitable mental models to execute them. I feel this is because most textbooks provide verbal descriptions of these algorithms and are often not specific enough for students to replicate reliably.

As a result, students lack the procedural memory to execute them confidently in an exam setting. This situation is also annoying as these questions often offer many easy marks if you know what you're doing.

This book hopes to redress the balance by working through, in a lot of detail, how these sorting and searching algorithms execute, which provides the basis for students to get comfortable with running and debugging their programs. I hope it is of use to you.

Yours sincerely,

Alfred M. Capone
`alfred.m.capone@gmail.com`

Part I

SORTING ALGORITHMS

Chapter 1
Insertion sort

1.1 Worked Example 1: Sorting a four element array

We start with the following unsorted array:

view	loop	bird	youth
0	1	2	3	4

and we want to sort it using insertion sort.

Inserting element number 0 (`view`)

We insert the item at index 0 in the input array (which is `view`) into the output array.

The output list is currently is empty, so `view` becomes the only element of the output array at the moment. Therefore the output array becomes:

view
0	1

Inserting element number 1 (`loop`)

We insert the item at index 1 in the input array (which is `loop`) into the output array.

The output array is currently:

view
0	1

Compare `loop` with element at index 0 in the current output array (which is `view`). We find that

$$\text{loop} \leq \text{view}$$

and therefore insert `loop` at position 0 in the output list.

The updated output array is now:

loop	view
0	1	2

Inserting element number 2 (bird)

We insert the item at index 2 in the input array (which is bird) into the output array.
The output array is currently:

loop	view
0	1	2

Compare bird with element at index 0 in the current output array (which is loop). We find that

$$bird \leq loop$$

and therefore insert bird at position 0 in the output list.
The updated output array is now:

bird	loop	view
0	1	2	3

Inserting element number 3 (youth)

We insert the item at index 3 in the input array (which is youth) into the output array.
The output array is currently:

bird	loop	view
0	1	2	3

Compare youth with element at index 0 in the current output array (which is bird). We find that

$$youth > bird,$$

therefore we can't insert yet.
Compare youth with element at index 1 in the current output array (which is loop). We find that

$$youth > loop,$$

therefore we can't insert yet.
Compare youth with element at index 2 in the current output array (which is view). We find that

$$\text{youth} > \text{view},$$

therefore we can't insert yet.

We see that youth is the largest item so we insert it at the end.
The updated output array is now:

bird	loop	view	youth
0	1	2	3	4

The final array is:

bird	loop	view	youth
0	1	2	3	4

1.2 Worked Example 2: Sorting a four element array

We start with the following unsorted array:

tube	queue	weed	note
0	1	2	3	4

and we want to sort it using insertion sort.

Inserting element number 0 (*tube*)

We insert the item at index 0 in the input array (which is tube) into the output array.
   The output list is currently is empty, so tube becomes the only element of the output array at the moment. Therefore the output array becomes:

tube
0	1

Inserting element number 1 (*queue*)

We insert the item at index 1 in the input array (which is queue) into the output array.
   The output array is currently:

tube
0	1

   Compare queue with element at index 0 in the current output array (which is tube). We find that

$$queue \leq tube$$

and therefore insert queue at position 0 in the output list.
   The updated output array is now:

queue	tube
0	1	2

Inserting element number 2 (*weed*)

We insert the item at index 2 in the input array (which is weed) into the output array.
   The output array is currently:

queue	tube
0	1	2

Compare weed with element at index 0 in the current output array (which is queue). We find that

$$\text{weed} > \text{queue},$$

therefore we can't insert yet.

Compare weed with element at index 1 in the current output array (which is tube). We find that

$$\text{weed} > \text{tube},$$

therefore we can't insert yet.

We see that weed is the largest item so we insert it at the end.

The updated output array is now:

queue	tube	weed
0	1	2	3

Inserting element number 3 (note)

We insert the item at index 3 in the input array (which is note) into the output array.

The output array is currently:

queue	tube	weed
0	1	2	3

Compare note with element at index 0 in the current output array (which is queue). We find that

$$\text{note} \leq \text{queue}$$

and therefore insert note at position 0 in the output list.

The updated output array is now:

note	queue	tube	weed
0	1	2	3	4

The final array is:

note	queue	tube	weed
0	1	2	3	4

1.3 Worked Example 3: Sorting a six element array

We start with the following unsorted array:

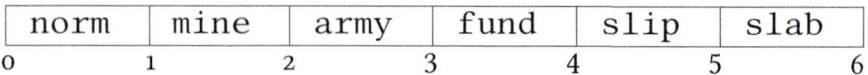

and we want to sort it using insertion sort.

Inserting element number 0 (norm)

We insert the item at index 0 in the input array (which is norm) into the output array.

The output list is currently is empty, so norm becomes the only element of the output array at the moment. Therefore the output array becomes:

norm
0   1

Inserting element number 1 (mine)

We insert the item at index 1 in the input array (which is mine) into the output array.

The output array is currently:

norm
0   1

Compare mine with element at index 0 in the current output array (which is norm). We find that

$$mine \leq norm$$

and therefore insert mine at position 0 in the output list.

The updated output array is now:

mine	norm
0	1 2

Inserting element number 2 (army)

We insert the item at index 2 in the input array (which is army) into the output array.

The output array is currently:

mine	norm
0	1 2

Compare `army` with element at index 0 in the current output array (which is `mine`). We find that

$$\text{army} \leq \text{mine}$$

and therefore insert `army` at position 0 in the output list.
The updated output array is now:

army	mine	norm
0	1	2
			3

Inserting element number 3 (fund)

We insert the item at index 3 in the input array (which is `fund`) into the output array.
The output array is currently:

army	mine	norm
0	1	2

Compare `fund` with element at index 0 in the current output array (which is `army`). We find that

$$\text{fund} > \text{army},$$

therefore we can't insert yet.
Compare `fund` with element at index 1 in the current output array (which is `mine`). We find that

$$\text{fund} \leq \text{mine}$$

and therefore insert `fund` at position 1 in the output list.
The updated output array is now:

army	fund	mine	norm
0	1	2	3

Inserting element number 4 (slip)

We insert the item at index 4 in the input array (which is `slip`) into the output array.
The output array is currently:

army	fund	mine	norm
0	1	2	3

Compare `slip` with element at index 0 in the current output array (which is `army`). We find that

$$\text{slip} > \text{army},$$

therefore we can't insert yet.

Compare `slip` with element at index 1 in the current output array (which is `fund`). We find that

$$\text{slip} > \text{fund},$$

therefore we can't insert yet.

Compare `slip` with element at index 2 in the current output array (which is `mine`). We find that

$$\text{slip} > \text{mine},$$

therefore we can't insert yet.

Compare `slip` with element at index 3 in the current output array (which is `norm`). We find that

$$\text{slip} > \text{norm},$$

therefore we can't insert yet.

We see that `slip` is the largest item so we insert it at the end.

The updated output array is now:

army	fund	mine	norm	slip
0	1	2	3	4	5

Inserting element number 5 (`slab`)

We insert the item at index 5 in the input array (which is `slab`) into the output array.

The output array is currently:

army	fund	mine	norm	slip
0	1	2	3	4	5

Compare `slab` with element at index 0 in the current output array (which is `army`). We find that

$$\text{slab} > \text{army},$$

therefore we can't insert yet.

Compare `slab` with element at index 1 in the current output array (which is `fund`). We find that

$$\text{slab} > \text{fund},$$

therefore we can't insert yet.

Compare `slab` with element at index 2 in the current output array (which is `mine`). We find that

$$\text{slab} > \text{mine},$$

therefore we can't insert yet.

Compare `slab` with element at index 3 in the current output array (which is `norm`). We find that

$$\text{slab} > \text{norm},$$

therefore we can't insert yet.

Compare `slab` with element at index 4 in the current output array (which is `slip`). We find that

$$\text{slab} \leq \text{slip}$$

and therefore insert `slab` at position 4 in the output list.
The updated output array is now:

army	fund	mine	norm	slab	slip	
0	1	2	3	4	5	6

The final array is:

army	fund	mine	norm	slab	slip	
0	1	2	3	4	5	6

1.4 Worked Example 4: Sorting a five element array

We start with the following unsorted array:

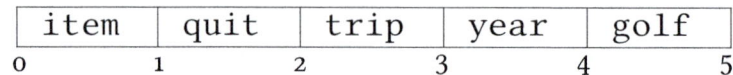

and we want to sort it using insertion sort.

Inserting element number 0 (`item`)

We insert the item at index 0 in the input array (which is `item`) into the output array.
  The output list is currently is empty, so `item` becomes the only element of the output array at the moment. Therefore the output array becomes:

item
0

Inserting element number 1 (`quit`)

We insert the item at index 1 in the input array (which is `quit`) into the output array.
  The output array is currently:

item
0

Compare `quit` with element at index 0 in the current output array (which is `item`). We find that

$$\text{quit} > \text{item},$$

therefore we can't insert yet.
  We see that `quit` is the largest item so we insert it at the end.
  The updated output array is now:

item	quit
0	1

Inserting element number 2 (`trip`)

We insert the item at index 2 in the input array (which is `trip`) into the output array.
  The output array is currently:

item	quit
0	1

Compare `trip` with element at index 0 in the current output array (which is `item`). We find that

$$\text{trip} > \text{item},$$

therefore we can't insert yet.

Compare `trip` with element at index 1 in the current output array (which is `quit`). We find that

$$\text{trip} > \text{quit},$$

therefore we can't insert yet.

We see that `trip` is the largest item so we insert it at the end.
The updated output array is now:

item	quit	trip	
0	1	2	3

Inserting element number 3 (year)

We insert the item at index 3 in the input array (which is `year`) into the output array.
The output array is currently:

item	quit	trip	
0	1	2	3

Compare `year` with element at index 0 in the current output array (which is `item`). We find that

$$\text{year} > \text{item},$$

therefore we can't insert yet.

Compare `year` with element at index 1 in the current output array (which is `quit`). We find that

$$\text{year} > \text{quit},$$

therefore we can't insert yet.

Compare `year` with element at index 2 in the current output array (which is `trip`). We find that

$$\text{year} > \text{trip},$$

therefore we can't insert yet.

We see that `year` is the largest item so we insert it at the end.
The updated output array is now:

item	quit	trip	year
0	1	2	3	4

Inserting element number 4 (golf)

We insert the item at index 4 in the input array (which is golf) into the output array.
The output array is currently:

item	quit	trip	year
0	1	2	3	4

Compare golf with element at index 0 in the current output array (which is item). We find that

$$golf \leq item$$

and therefore insert golf at position 0 in the output list.
The updated output array is now:

golf	item	quit	trip	year
0	1	2	3	4	5

The final array is:

golf	item	quit	trip	year
0	1	2	3	4	5

Exercises in Sorting and Searching

1.5 Worked Example 5: Sorting a seven element array

We start with the following unsorted array:

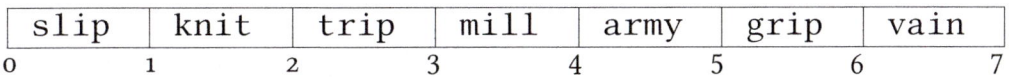

and we want to sort it using insertion sort.

Inserting element number 0 (slip)

We insert the item at index 0 in the input array (which is slip) into the output array.

The output list is currently is empty, so slip becomes the only element of the output array at the moment. Therefore the output array becomes:

slip
0

Inserting element number 1 (knit)

We insert the item at index 1 in the input array (which is knit) into the output array.
The output array is currently:

slip
0

Compare knit with element at index 0 in the current output array (which is slip). We find that

$$knit \leq slip$$

and therefore insert knit at position 0 in the output list.
The updated output array is now:

knit	slip
0	1

Inserting element number 2 (trip)

We insert the item at index 2 in the input array (which is trip) into the output array.
The output array is currently:

knit	slip
0	1

21 | 123

Compare `trip` with element at index 0 in the current output array (which is `knit`). We find that

$$trip > knit,$$

therefore we can't insert yet.

Compare `trip` with element at index 1 in the current output array (which is `slip`). We find that

$$trip > slip,$$

therefore we can't insert yet.

We see that `trip` is the largest item so we insert it at the end.

The updated output array is now:

knit	slip	trip
0	1	2	3

Inserting element number 3 (`mill`)

We insert the item at index 3 in the input array (which is `mill`) into the output array.

The output array is currently:

knit	slip	trip
0	1	2	3

Compare `mill` with element at index 0 in the current output array (which is `knit`). We find that

$$mill > knit,$$

therefore we can't insert yet.

Compare `mill` with element at index 1 in the current output array (which is `slip`). We find that

$$mill \leq slip$$

and therefore insert `mill` at position 1 in the output list.

The updated output array is now:

knit	mill	slip	trip
0	1	2	3	4

Inserting element number 4 (army)

We insert the item at index 4 in the input array (which is army) into the output array.
The output array is currently:

knit	mill	slip	trip	
0	1	2	3	4

Compare army with element at index 0 in the current output array (which is knit). We find that

$$army \leq knit$$

and therefore insert army at position 0 in the output list.
The updated output array is now:

army	knit	mill	slip	trip	
0	1	2	3	4	5

Inserting element number 5 (grip)

We insert the item at index 5 in the input array (which is grip) into the output array.
The output array is currently:

army	knit	mill	slip	trip	
0	1	2	3	4	5

Compare grip with element at index 0 in the current output array (which is army). We find that

$$grip > army,$$

therefore we can't insert yet.
Compare grip with element at index 1 in the current output array (which is knit). We find that

$$grip \leq knit$$

and therefore insert grip at position 1 in the output list.
The updated output array is now:

army	grip	knit	mill	slip	trip	
0	1	2	3	4	5	6

Inserting element number 6 (vain)

We insert the item at index 6 in the input array (which is vain) into the output array.

The output array is currently:

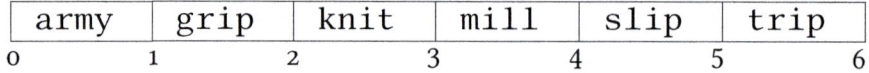

Compare vain with element at index 0 in the current output array (which is army). We find that

$$vain > army,$$

therefore we can't insert yet.

Compare vain with element at index 1 in the current output array (which is grip). We find that

$$vain > grip,$$

therefore we can't insert yet.

Compare vain with element at index 2 in the current output array (which is knit). We find that

$$vain > knit,$$

therefore we can't insert yet.

Compare vain with element at index 3 in the current output array (which is mill). We find that

$$vain > mill,$$

therefore we can't insert yet.

Compare vain with element at index 4 in the current output array (which is slip). We find that

$$vain > slip,$$

therefore we can't insert yet.

Compare vain with element at index 5 in the current output array (which is trip). We find that

$$vain > trip,$$

therefore we can't insert yet.

We see that vain is the largest item so we insert it at the end.

The updated output array is now:

Exercises in Sorting and Searching

army	grip	knit	mill	slip	trip	vain
0	1	2	3	4	5	6	7

The final array is:

army	grip	knit	mill	slip	trip	vain
0	1	2	3	4	5	6	7

1.6 Worked Example 6: Sorting a five element array

We start with the following unsorted array:

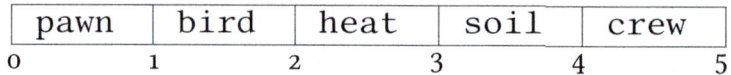

and we want to sort it using insertion sort.

Inserting element number 0 (pawn)

We insert the item at index 0 in the input array (which is pawn) into the output array.

The output list is currently is empty, so pawn becomes the only element of the output array at the moment. Therefore the output array becomes:

pawn
0 1

Inserting element number 1 (bird)

We insert the item at index 1 in the input array (which is bird) into the output array.

The output array is currently:

pawn
0 1

Compare bird with element at index 0 in the current output array (which is pawn). We find that

$$bird \leq pawn$$

and therefore insert bird at position 0 in the output list.
The updated output array is now:

bird	pawn
0	1 2

Inserting element number 2 (heat)

We insert the item at index 2 in the input array (which is heat) into the output array.
The output array is currently:

bird	pawn
0	1 2

Compare heat with element at index 0 in the current output array (which is bird). We find that

$$\text{heat} > \text{bird},$$

therefore we can't insert yet.

Compare heat with element at index 1 in the current output array (which is pawn). We find that

$$\text{heat} \leq \text{pawn}$$

and therefore insert heat at position 1 in the output list.
The updated output array is now:

bird	heat	pawn	
0	1	2	3

Inserting element number 3 (soil)

We insert the item at index 3 in the input array (which is soil) into the output array.
The output array is currently:

bird	heat	pawn	
0	1	2	3

Compare soil with element at index 0 in the current output array (which is bird). We find that

$$\text{soil} > \text{bird},$$

therefore we can't insert yet.

Compare soil with element at index 1 in the current output array (which is heat). We find that

$$\text{soil} > \text{heat},$$

therefore we can't insert yet.

Compare soil with element at index 2 in the current output array (which is pawn). We find that

$$\text{soil} > \text{pawn},$$

therefore we can't insert yet.

We see that soil is the largest item so we insert it at the end.
The updated output array is now:

bird	heat	pawn	soil	
0	1	2	3	4

Inserting element number 4 (crew)

We insert the item at index 4 in the input array (which is crew) into the output array.
The output array is currently:

bird	heat	pawn	soil
0	1	2	3	4

Compare crew with element at index 0 in the current output array (which is bird). We find that

$$crew > bird,$$

therefore we can't insert yet.
Compare crew with element at index 1 in the current output array (which is heat). We find that

$$crew \leq heat$$

and therefore insert crew at position 1 in the output list.
The updated output array is now:

bird	crew	heat	pawn	soil
0	1	2	3	4	5

The final array is:

bird	crew	heat	pawn	soil
0	1	2	3	4	5

1.7 Worked Example 7: Sorting a four element array

We start with the following unsorted array:

foot	like	view	iron
0	1	2	3	4

and we want to sort it using insertion sort.

Inserting element number 0 (foot)

We insert the item at index 0 in the input array (which is foot) into the output array.

The output list is currently is empty, so foot becomes the only element of the output array at the moment. Therefore the output array becomes:

foot
0	1

Inserting element number 1 (like)

We insert the item at index 1 in the input array (which is like) into the output array.
The output array is currently:

foot
0	1

Compare like with element at index 0 in the current output array (which is foot). We find that

$$like > foot,$$

therefore we can't insert yet.
We see that like is the largest item so we insert it at the end.
The updated output array is now:

foot	like
0	1	2

Inserting element number 2 (view)

We insert the item at index 2 in the input array (which is view) into the output array.
The output array is currently:

foot	like
0	1	2

29 | 123

Compare `view` with element at index 0 in the current output array (which is `foot`). We find that

$$\text{view} > \text{foot},$$

therefore we can't insert yet.

Compare `view` with element at index 1 in the current output array (which is `like`). We find that

$$\text{view} > \text{like},$$

therefore we can't insert yet.

We see that `view` is the largest item so we insert it at the end.

The updated output array is now:

foot	like	view
0	1	2	3

Inserting element number 3 (`iron`)

We insert the item at index 3 in the input array (which is `iron`) into the output array.

The output array is currently:

foot	like	view
0	1	2	3

Compare `iron` with element at index 0 in the current output array (which is `foot`). We find that

$$\text{iron} > \text{foot},$$

therefore we can't insert yet.

Compare `iron` with element at index 1 in the current output array (which is `like`). We find that

$$\text{iron} \leq \text{like}$$

and therefore insert `iron` at position 1 in the output list.

The updated output array is now:

foot	iron	like	view
0	1	2	3	4

The final array is:

foot	iron	like	view
0	1	2	3	4

Exercises in Sorting and Searching

1.8 Worked Example 8: Sorting a seven element array

We start with the following unsorted array:

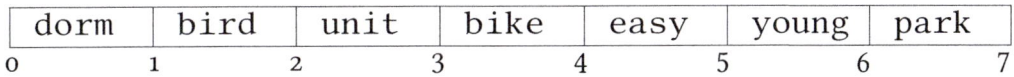

and we want to sort it using insertion sort.

Inserting element number 0 (dorm)

We insert the item at index 0 in the input array (which is dorm) into the output array.

The output list is currently is empty, so dorm becomes the only element of the output array at the moment. Therefore the output array becomes:

dorm
0   1

Inserting element number 1 (bird)

We insert the item at index 1 in the input array (which is bird) into the output array.
The output array is currently:

dorm
0   1

Compare bird with element at index 0 in the current output array (which is dorm). We find that

$$bird \leq dorm$$

and therefore insert bird at position 0 in the output list.
The updated output array is now:

bird	dorm
0	1 2

Inserting element number 2 (unit)

We insert the item at index 2 in the input array (which is unit) into the output array.
The output array is currently:

bird	dorm
0	1 2

Compare `unit` with element at index 0 in the current output array (which is `bird`). We find that

$$\text{unit} > \text{bird},$$

therefore we can't insert yet.

Compare `unit` with element at index 1 in the current output array (which is `dorm`). We find that

$$\text{unit} > \text{dorm},$$

therefore we can't insert yet.

We see that `unit` is the largest item so we insert it at the end.

The updated output array is now:

bird	dorm	unit
0	1	2	3

Inserting element number 3 (`bike`)

We insert the item at index 3 in the input array (which is `bike`) into the output array.

The output array is currently:

bird	dorm	unit
0	1	2	3

Compare `bike` with element at index 0 in the current output array (which is `bird`). We find that

$$\text{bike} \leq \text{bird}$$

and therefore insert `bike` at position 0 in the output list.

The updated output array is now:

bike	bird	dorm	unit
0	1	2	3	4

Inserting element number 4 (`easy`)

We insert the item at index 4 in the input array (which is `easy`) into the output array.

The output array is currently:

bike	bird	dorm	unit
0	1	2	3	4

Exercises in Sorting and Searching

Compare easy with element at index 0 in the current output array (which is bike). We find that

$$easy > bike,$$

therefore we can't insert yet.

Compare easy with element at index 1 in the current output array (which is bird). We find that

$$easy > bird,$$

therefore we can't insert yet.

Compare easy with element at index 2 in the current output array (which is dorm). We find that

$$easy > dorm,$$

therefore we can't insert yet.

Compare easy with element at index 3 in the current output array (which is unit). We find that

$$easy \leq unit$$

and therefore insert easy at position 3 in the output list.
The updated output array is now:

bike	bird	dorm	easy	unit	
0	1	2	3	4	5

Inserting element number 5 (young)

We insert the item at index 5 in the input array (which is young) into the output array.
The output array is currently:

bike	bird	dorm	easy	unit	
0	1	2	3	4	5

Compare young with element at index 0 in the current output array (which is bike). We find that

$$young > bike,$$

therefore we can't insert yet.

Compare young with element at index 1 in the current output array (which is bird). We find that

$$\text{young} > \text{bird},$$

therefore we can't insert yet.

Compare young with element at index 2 in the current output array (which is dorm). We find that

$$\text{young} > \text{dorm},$$

therefore we can't insert yet.

Compare young with element at index 3 in the current output array (which is easy). We find that

$$\text{young} > \text{easy},$$

therefore we can't insert yet.

Compare young with element at index 4 in the current output array (which is unit). We find that

$$\text{young} > \text{unit},$$

therefore we can't insert yet.

We see that young is the largest item so we insert it at the end.

The updated output array is now:

bike	bird	dorm	easy	unit	young
0	1	2	3	4	5	6

Inserting element number 6 (park)

We insert the item at index 6 in the input array (which is park) into the output array.

The output array is currently:

bike	bird	dorm	easy	unit	young
0	1	2	3	4	5	6

Compare park with element at index 0 in the current output array (which is bike). We find that

$$\text{park} > \text{bike},$$

therefore we can't insert yet.

Compare park with element at index 1 in the current output array (which is bird). We find that

$$\text{park} > \text{bird},$$

Exercises in Sorting and Searching

therefore we can't insert yet.

Compare park with element at index 2 in the current output array (which is dorm). We find that

$$\text{park} > \text{dorm},$$

therefore we can't insert yet.

Compare park with element at index 3 in the current output array (which is easy). We find that

$$\text{park} > \text{easy},$$

therefore we can't insert yet.

Compare park with element at index 4 in the current output array (which is unit). We find that

$$\text{park} \leq \text{unit}$$

and therefore insert park at position 4 in the output list. The updated output array is now:

bike	bird	dorm	easy	park	unit	young
0	1	2	3	4	5	6 7

The final array is:

bike	bird	dorm	easy	park	unit	young
0	1	2	3	4	5	6 7

Chapter 2
Bubble sort

2.1 Worked Example 1: Sorting a five element array (in three passes)

We start with the input array:

view	loop	bird	youth	tube
0	1	2	3	4

and want to sort it using bubblesort.

Pass number 1
The array currently looks like this:

view	loop	bird	youth	tube
0	1	2	3	4

- We look at elements at indices 0 and 1, and compare view with loop.

  Outcome: view $\geq$ loop, therefore we swap them.

  Current array:

loop	view	bird	youth	tube
0	1	2	3	4

- We look at elements at indices 1 and 2, and compare view with bird.

  Outcome: view $\geq$ bird, therefore we swap them.

  Current array:

loop	bird	view	youth	tube
0	1	2	3	4

- We look at elements at indices 2 and 3, and compare `view` with `youth`.
  Outcome: `view` ≤ `youth`, therefore no swap is needed.

- We look at elements at indices 3 and 4, and compare `youth` with `tube`.
  Outcome: `youth` ≥ `tube`, therefore we swap them.
  Current array:

loop	bird	view	tube	youth
0	1	2	3	4	5

In this pass, a swap was performed, so we have to do another pass.

Pass number 2

The array currently looks like this:

loop	bird	view	tube	youth
0	1	2	3	4	5

- We look at elements at indices 0 and 1, and compare `loop` with `bird`.
  Outcome: `loop` ≥ `bird`, therefore we swap them.
  Current array:

bird	loop	view	tube	youth
0	1	2	3	4	5

- We look at elements at indices 1 and 2, and compare `loop` with `view`.
  Outcome: `loop` ≤ `view`, therefore no swap is needed.

- We look at elements at indices 2 and 3, and compare `view` with `tube`.
  Outcome: `view` ≥ `tube`, therefore we swap them.
  Current array:

bird	loop	tube	view	youth
0	1	2	3	4	5

- We look at elements at indices 3 and 4, and compare `view` with `youth`.
  Outcome: `view` ≤ `youth`, therefore no swap is needed.

In this pass, a swap was performed, so we have to do another pass.

Exercises in Sorting and Searching

Pass number 3

The array currently looks like this:

bird	loop	tube	view	youth	
0	1	2	3	4	5

- We look at elements at indices 0 and 1, and compare bird with loop.
  Outcome: bird $\leq$ loop, therefore no swap is needed.

- We look at elements at indices 1 and 2, and compare loop with tube.
  Outcome: loop $\leq$ tube, therefore no swap is needed.

- We look at elements at indices 2 and 3, and compare tube with view.
  Outcome: tube $\leq$ view, therefore no swap is needed.

- We look at elements at indices 3 and 4, and compare view with youth.
  Outcome: view $\leq$ youth, therefore no swap is needed.

No swaps were performed in this pass, so we are done.
Final array:

bird	loop	tube	view	youth	
0	1	2	3	4	5

2.2 Worked Example 2: Sorting an seven element array (in six passes)

We start with the input array:

weed	note	user	pace	item	norm	mine	
0	1	2	3	4	5	6	7

and want to sort it using bubblesort.

Pass number 1

The array currently looks like this:

weed	note	user	pace	item	norm	mine	
0	1	2	3	4	5	6	7

- We look at elements at indices 0 and 1, and compare weed with note.

  Outcome: weed $\geq$ note, therefore we swap them.

  Current array:

note	weed	user	pace	item	norm	mine	
0	1	2	3	4	5	6	7

- We look at elements at indices 1 and 2, and compare weed with user.

  Outcome: weed $\geq$ user, therefore we swap them.

  Current array:

note	user	weed	pace	item	norm	mine	
0	1	2	3	4	5	6	7

- We look at elements at indices 2 and 3, and compare weed with pace.

  Outcome: weed $\geq$ pace, therefore we swap them.

  Current array:

note	user	pace	weed	item	norm	mine	
0	1	2	3	4	5	6	7

- We look at elements at indices 3 and 4, and compare weed with item.

  Outcome: weed $\geq$ item, therefore we swap them.

  Current array:

note	user	pace	item	weed	norm	mine	
0	1	2	3	4	5	6	7

Exercises in Sorting and Searching

- We look at elements at indices 4 and 5, and compare weed with norm.

  Outcome: weed ≥ norm, therefore we swap them.

  Current array:

note	user	pace	item	norm	weed	mine
0	1	2	3	4	5	6	7

- We look at elements at indices 5 and 6, and compare weed with mine.

  Outcome: weed ≥ mine, therefore we swap them.

  Current array:

note	user	pace	item	norm	mine	weed
0	1	2	3	4	5	6	7

In this pass, a swap was performed, so we have to do another pass.

Pass number 2

The array currently looks like this:

note	user	pace	item	norm	mine	weed
0	1	2	3	4	5	6	7

- We look at elements at indices 0 and 1, and compare note with user.

  Outcome: note ≤ user, therefore no swap is needed.

- We look at elements at indices 1 and 2, and compare user with pace.

  Outcome: user ≥ pace, therefore we swap them.

  Current array:

note	pace	user	item	norm	mine	weed
0	1	2	3	4	5	6	7

- We look at elements at indices 2 and 3, and compare user with item.

  Outcome: user ≥ item, therefore we swap them.

  Current array:

note	pace	item	user	norm	mine	weed
0	1	2	3	4	5	6	7

41 | 123

- We look at elements at indices 3 and 4, and compare user with norm.

  Outcome: user ≥ norm, therefore we swap them.

  Current array:

note	pace	item	norm	user	mine	weed
0	1	2	3	4	5	6	7

- We look at elements at indices 4 and 5, and compare user with mine.

  Outcome: user ≥ mine, therefore we swap them.

  Current array:

note	pace	item	norm	mine	user	weed
0	1	2	3	4	5	6	7

- We look at elements at indices 5 and 6, and compare user with weed.

  Outcome: user ≤ weed, therefore no swap is needed.

In this pass, a swap was performed, so we have to do another pass.

Pass number 3

The array currently looks like this:

note	pace	item	norm	mine	user	weed
0	1	2	3	4	5	6	7

- We look at elements at indices 0 and 1, and compare note with pace.

  Outcome: note ≤ pace, therefore no swap is needed.

- We look at elements at indices 1 and 2, and compare pace with item.

  Outcome: pace ≥ item, therefore we swap them.

  Current array:

note	item	pace	norm	mine	user	weed
0	1	2	3	4	5	6	7

- We look at elements at indices 2 and 3, and compare pace with norm.

  Outcome: pace ≥ norm, therefore we swap them.

  Current array:

note	item	norm	pace	mine	user	weed
0	1	2	3	4	5	6	7

Exercises in Sorting and Searching

- We look at elements at indices 3 and 4, and compare pace with mine.

  Outcome: pace ≥ mine, therefore we swap them.

  Current array:

note	item	norm	mine	pace	user	weed
0	1	2	3	4	5	6	7

- We look at elements at indices 4 and 5, and compare pace with user.

  Outcome: pace ≤ user, therefore no swap is needed.

- We look at elements at indices 5 and 6, and compare user with weed.

  Outcome: user ≤ weed, therefore no swap is needed.

In this pass, a swap was performed, so we have to do another pass.

Pass number 4

The array currently looks like this:

note	item	norm	mine	pace	user	weed
0	1	2	3	4	5	6	7

- We look at elements at indices 0 and 1, and compare note with item.

  Outcome: note ≥ item, therefore we swap them.

  Current array:

item	note	norm	mine	pace	user	weed
0	1	2	3	4	5	6	7

- We look at elements at indices 1 and 2, and compare note with norm.

  Outcome: note ≥ norm, therefore we swap them.

  Current array:

item	norm	note	mine	pace	user	weed
0	1	2	3	4	5	6	7

- We look at elements at indices 2 and 3, and compare note with mine.

  Outcome: note ≥ mine, therefore we swap them.

  Current array:

item	norm	mine	note	pace	user	weed
0	1	2	3	4	5	6	7

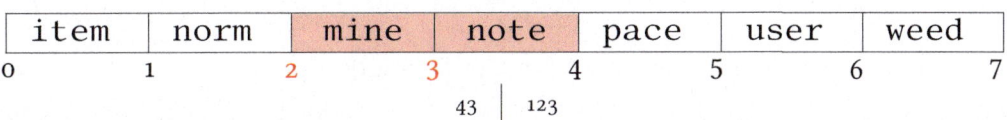

- We look at elements at indices 3 and 4, and compare `note` with `pace`.
  Outcome: `note` $\leq$ `pace`, therefore no swap is needed.

- We look at elements at indices 4 and 5, and compare `pace` with `user`.
  Outcome: `pace` $\leq$ `user`, therefore no swap is needed.

- We look at elements at indices 5 and 6, and compare `user` with `weed`.
  Outcome: `user` $\leq$ `weed`, therefore no swap is needed.

In this pass, a swap was performed, so we have to do another pass.

Pass number 5

The array currently looks like this:

item	norm	mine	note	pace	user	weed	
0	1	2	3	4	5	6	7

- We look at elements at indices 0 and 1, and compare `item` with `norm`.
  Outcome: `item` $\leq$ `norm`, therefore no swap is needed.

- We look at elements at indices 1 and 2, and compare `norm` with `mine`.
  Outcome: `norm` $\geq$ `mine`, therefore we swap them.
  Current array:

item	mine	norm	note	pace	user	weed	
0	1	2	3	4	5	6	7

- We look at elements at indices 2 and 3, and compare `norm` with `note`.
  Outcome: `norm` $\leq$ `note`, therefore no swap is needed.

- We look at elements at indices 3 and 4, and compare `note` with `pace`.
  Outcome: `note` $\leq$ `pace`, therefore no swap is needed.

- We look at elements at indices 4 and 5, and compare `pace` with `user`.
  Outcome: `pace` $\leq$ `user`, therefore no swap is needed.

- We look at elements at indices 5 and 6, and compare `user` with `weed`.
  Outcome: `user` $\leq$ `weed`, therefore no swap is needed.

In this pass, a swap was performed, so we have to do another pass.

Exercises in Sorting and Searching

Pass number 6
The array currently looks like this:

item	mine	norm	note	pace	user	weed	
0	1	2	3	4	5	6	7

- We look at elements at indices 0 and 1, and compare item with mine.
  Outcome: item ≤ mine, therefore no swap is needed.

- We look at elements at indices 1 and 2, and compare mine with norm.
  Outcome: mine ≤ norm, therefore no swap is needed.

- We look at elements at indices 2 and 3, and compare norm with note.
  Outcome: norm ≤ note, therefore no swap is needed.

- We look at elements at indices 3 and 4, and compare note with pace.
  Outcome: note ≤ pace, therefore no swap is needed.

- We look at elements at indices 4 and 5, and compare pace with user.
  Outcome: pace ≤ user, therefore no swap is needed.

- We look at elements at indices 5 and 6, and compare user with weed.
  Outcome: user ≤ weed, therefore no swap is needed.

No swaps were performed in this pass, so we are done.
Final array:

item	mine	norm	note	pace	user	weed	
0	1	2	3	4	5	6	7

2.3 Worked Example 3: Sorting a five element array (in five passes)

We start with the input array:

fund	slip	slab	riot	edge
0	1	2	3	4	5

and want to sort it using bubblesort.

Pass number 1

The array currently looks like this:

fund	slip	slab	riot	edge
0	1	2	3	4	5

- We look at elements at indices 0 and 1, and compare fund with slip.
  Outcome: fund $\leq$ slip, therefore no swap is needed.

- We look at elements at indices 1 and 2, and compare slip with slab.
  Outcome: slip $\geq$ slab, therefore we swap them.
  Current array:

fund	slab	slip	riot	edge
0	1	2	3	4	5

- We look at elements at indices 2 and 3, and compare slip with riot.
  Outcome: slip $\geq$ riot, therefore we swap them.
  Current array:

fund	slab	riot	slip	edge
0	1	2	3	4	5

- We look at elements at indices 3 and 4, and compare slip with edge.
  Outcome: slip $\geq$ edge, therefore we swap them.
  Current array:

fund	slab	riot	edge	slip
0	1	2	3	4	5

In this pass, a swap was performed, so we have to do another pass.

Exercises in Sorting and Searching

Pass number 2
The array currently looks like this:

fund	slab	riot	edge	slip
0	1	2	3	4	5

- We look at elements at indices 0 and 1, and compare fund with slab.
  Outcome: fund ≤ slab, therefore no swap is needed.

- We look at elements at indices 1 and 2, and compare slab with riot.
  Outcome: slab ≥ riot, therefore we swap them.
  Current array:

fund	riot	slab	edge	slip
0	1	2	3	4	5

- We look at elements at indices 2 and 3, and compare slab with edge.
  Outcome: slab ≥ edge, therefore we swap them.
  Current array:

fund	riot	edge	slab	slip
0	1	2	3	4	5

- We look at elements at indices 3 and 4, and compare slab with slip.
  Outcome: slab ≤ slip, therefore no swap is needed.

In this pass, a swap was performed, so we have to do another pass.

Pass number 3
The array currently looks like this:

fund	riot	edge	slab	slip
0	1	2	3	4	5

- We look at elements at indices 0 and 1, and compare fund with riot.
  Outcome: fund ≤ riot, therefore no swap is needed.

- We look at elements at indices 1 and 2, and compare riot with edge.
  Outcome: riot ≥ edge, therefore we swap them.
  Current array:

fund	edge	riot	slab	slip
0	1	2	3	4	5

- We look at elements at indices 2 and 3, and compare `riot` with `slab`.
  Outcome: $\text{riot} \leq \text{slab}$, therefore no swap is needed.

- We look at elements at indices 3 and 4, and compare `slab` with `slip`.
  Outcome: $\text{slab} \leq \text{slip}$, therefore no swap is needed.

In this pass, a swap was performed, so we have to do another pass.

Pass number 4

The array currently looks like this:

fund	edge	riot	slab	slip
0	1	2	3	4	5

- We look at elements at indices 0 and 1, and compare `fund` with `edge`.
  Outcome: $\text{fund} \geq \text{edge}$, therefore we swap them.
  Current array:

edge	fund	riot	slab	slip
0	1	2	3	4	5

- We look at elements at indices 1 and 2, and compare `fund` with `riot`.
  Outcome: $\text{fund} \leq \text{riot}$, therefore no swap is needed.

- We look at elements at indices 2 and 3, and compare `riot` with `slab`.
  Outcome: $\text{riot} \leq \text{slab}$, therefore no swap is needed.

- We look at elements at indices 3 and 4, and compare `slab` with `slip`.
  Outcome: $\text{slab} \leq \text{slip}$, therefore no swap is needed.

In this pass, a swap was performed, so we have to do another pass.

Pass number 5

The array currently looks like this:

edge	fund	riot	slab	slip
0	1	2	3	4	5

- We look at elements at indices 0 and 1, and compare `edge` with `fund`.
  Outcome: $\text{edge} \leq \text{fund}$, therefore no swap is needed.

Exercises in Sorting and Searching

- We look at elements at indices 1 and 2, and compare fund with riot.
  Outcome: fund $\leq$ riot, therefore no swap is needed.

- We look at elements at indices 2 and 3, and compare riot with slab.
  Outcome: riot $\leq$ slab, therefore no swap is needed.

- We look at elements at indices 3 and 4, and compare slab with slip.
  Outcome: slab $\leq$ slip, therefore no swap is needed.

No swaps were performed in this pass, so we are done.
Final array:

edge	fund	riot	slab	slip
0	1	2	3	4

2.4 Worked Example 4: Sorting a six element array (in five passes)

We start with the input array:

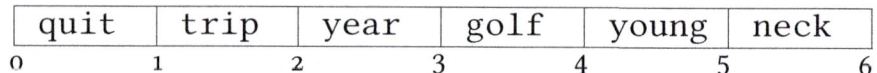

and want to sort it using bubblesort.

Pass number 1

The array currently looks like this:

quit	trip	year	golf	young	neck
0	1	2	3	4	5

- We look at elements at indices 0 and 1, and compare quit with trip.
  Outcome: quit $\leq$ trip, therefore no swap is needed.

- We look at elements at indices 1 and 2, and compare trip with year.
  Outcome: trip $\leq$ year, therefore no swap is needed.

- We look at elements at indices 2 and 3, and compare year with golf.
  Outcome: year $\geq$ golf, therefore we swap them.
  Current array:

quit	trip	golf	year	young	neck
0	1	2	3	4	5

- We look at elements at indices 3 and 4, and compare year with young.
  Outcome: year $\leq$ young, therefore no swap is needed.

- We look at elements at indices 4 and 5, and compare young with neck.
  Outcome: young $\geq$ neck, therefore we swap them.
  Current array:

quit	trip	golf	year	neck	young
0	1	2	3	4	5

In this pass, a swap was performed, so we have to do another pass.

Exercises in Sorting and Searching

Pass number 2

The array currently looks like this:

quit	trip	golf	year	neck	young
0	1	2	3	4	5	6

- We look at elements at indices 0 and 1, and compare quit with trip.
  Outcome: quit $\leq$ trip, therefore no swap is needed.

- We look at elements at indices 1 and 2, and compare trip with golf.
  Outcome: trip $\geq$ golf, therefore we swap them.
  Current array:

quit	golf	trip	year	neck	young
0	1	2	3	4	5	6

- We look at elements at indices 2 and 3, and compare trip with year.
  Outcome: trip $\leq$ year, therefore no swap is needed.

- We look at elements at indices 3 and 4, and compare year with neck.
  Outcome: year $\geq$ neck, therefore we swap them.
  Current array:

quit	golf	trip	neck	year	young
0	1	2	3	4	5	6

- We look at elements at indices 4 and 5, and compare year with young.
  Outcome: year $\leq$ young, therefore no swap is needed.

In this pass, a swap was performed, so we have to do another pass.

Pass number 3

The array currently looks like this:

quit	golf	trip	neck	year	young
0	1	2	3	4	5	6

- We look at elements at indices 0 and 1, and compare quit with golf.
  Outcome: quit $\geq$ golf, therefore we swap them.
  Current array:

golf	quit	trip	neck	year	young
0	1	2	3	4	5	6

- We look at elements at indices 1 and 2, and compare `quit` with `trip`.
  Outcome: `quit` ≤ `trip`, therefore no swap is needed.
- We look at elements at indices 2 and 3, and compare `trip` with `neck`.
  Outcome: `trip` ≥ `neck`, therefore we swap them.
  Current array:

golf	quit	neck	trip	year	young
0	1	2	3	4	5	6

- We look at elements at indices 3 and 4, and compare `trip` with `year`.
  Outcome: `trip` ≤ `year`, therefore no swap is needed.
- We look at elements at indices 4 and 5, and compare `year` with `young`.
  Outcome: `year` ≤ `young`, therefore no swap is needed.

In this pass, a swap was performed, so we have to do another pass.

Pass number 4

The array currently looks like this:

golf	quit	neck	trip	year	young
0	1	2	3	4	5	6

- We look at elements at indices 0 and 1, and compare `golf` with `quit`.
  Outcome: `golf` ≤ `quit`, therefore no swap is needed.
- We look at elements at indices 1 and 2, and compare `quit` with `neck`.
  Outcome: `quit` ≥ `neck`, therefore we swap them.
  Current array:

golf	neck	quit	trip	year	young
0	1	2	3	4	5	6

- We look at elements at indices 2 and 3, and compare `quit` with `trip`.
  Outcome: `quit` ≤ `trip`, therefore no swap is needed.
- We look at elements at indices 3 and 4, and compare `trip` with `year`.
  Outcome: `trip` ≤ `year`, therefore no swap is needed.
- We look at elements at indices 4 and 5, and compare `year` with `young`.
  Outcome: `year` ≤ `young`, therefore no swap is needed.

In this pass, a swap was performed, so we have to do another pass.

Pass number 5

The array currently looks like this:

golf	neck	quit	trip	year	young	
0	1	2	3	4	5	6

- We look at elements at indices 0 and 1, and compare golf with neck.
  Outcome: golf ≤ neck, therefore no swap is needed.

- We look at elements at indices 1 and 2, and compare neck with quit.
  Outcome: neck ≤ quit, therefore no swap is needed.

- We look at elements at indices 2 and 3, and compare quit with trip.
  Outcome: quit ≤ trip, therefore no swap is needed.

- We look at elements at indices 3 and 4, and compare trip with year.
  Outcome: trip ≤ year, therefore no swap is needed.

- We look at elements at indices 4 and 5, and compare year with young.
  Outcome: year ≤ young, therefore no swap is needed.

No swaps were performed in this pass, so we are done.
Final array:

golf	neck	quit	trip	year	young	
0	1	2	3	4	5	6

2.5 Worked Example 5: Sorting a six element array (in five passes)

We start with the input array:

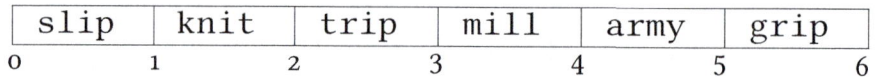

and want to sort it using bubblesort.

Pass number 1

The array currently looks like this:

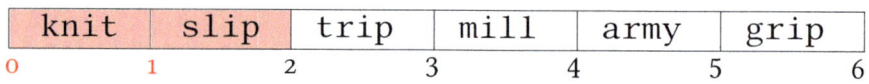

- We look at elements at indices 0 and 1, and compare slip with knit.

  Outcome: slip ≥ knit, therefore we swap them.

  Current array:

knit	slip	trip	mill	army	grip
0	1	2	3	4	5

- We look at elements at indices 1 and 2, and compare slip with trip.

  Outcome: slip ≤ trip, therefore no swap is needed.

- We look at elements at indices 2 and 3, and compare trip with mill.

  Outcome: trip ≥ mill, therefore we swap them.

  Current array:

knit	slip	mill	trip	army	grip
0	1	2	3	4	5

- We look at elements at indices 3 and 4, and compare trip with army.

  Outcome: trip ≥ army, therefore we swap them.

  Current array:

  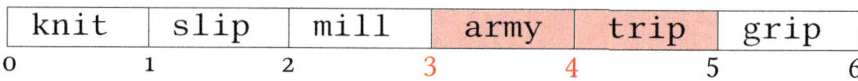

Exercises in Sorting and Searching

- We look at elements at indices 4 and 5, and compare trip with grip.
  Outcome: trip $\geq$ grip, therefore we swap them.
  Current array:

knit	slip	mill	army	grip	trip
0	1	2	3	4	5	6

In this pass, a swap was performed, so we have to do another pass.

Pass number 2

The array currently looks like this:

knit	slip	mill	army	grip	trip
0	1	2	3	4	5	6

- We look at elements at indices 0 and 1, and compare knit with slip.
  Outcome: knit $\leq$ slip, therefore no swap is needed.

- We look at elements at indices 1 and 2, and compare slip with mill.
  Outcome: slip $\geq$ mill, therefore we swap them.
  Current array:

knit	mill	slip	army	grip	trip
0	1	2	3	4	5	6

- We look at elements at indices 2 and 3, and compare slip with army.
  Outcome: slip $\geq$ army, therefore we swap them.
  Current array:

knit	mill	army	slip	grip	trip
0	1	2	3	4	5	6

- We look at elements at indices 3 and 4, and compare slip with grip.
  Outcome: slip $\geq$ grip, therefore we swap them.
  Current array:

knit	mill	army	grip	slip	trip
0	1	2	3	4	5	6

- We look at elements at indices 4 and 5, and compare slip with trip.
  Outcome: slip $\leq$ trip, therefore no swap is needed.

In this pass, a swap was performed, so we have to do another pass.

Pass number 3

The array currently looks like this:

knit	mill	army	grip	slip	trip
0	1	2	3	4	5	6

- We look at elements at indices 0 and 1, and compare knit with mill.
  Outcome: knit ≤ mill, therefore no swap is needed.

- We look at elements at indices 1 and 2, and compare mill with army.
  Outcome: mill ≥ army, therefore we swap them.
  Current array:

knit	army	mill	grip	slip	trip
0	1	2	3	4	5	6

- We look at elements at indices 2 and 3, and compare mill with grip.
  Outcome: mill ≥ grip, therefore we swap them.
  Current array:

knit	army	grip	mill	slip	trip
0	1	2	3	4	5	6

- We look at elements at indices 3 and 4, and compare mill with slip.
  Outcome: mill ≤ slip, therefore no swap is needed.

- We look at elements at indices 4 and 5, and compare slip with trip.
  Outcome: slip ≤ trip, therefore no swap is needed.

In this pass, a swap was performed, so we have to do another pass.

Pass number 4

The array currently looks like this:

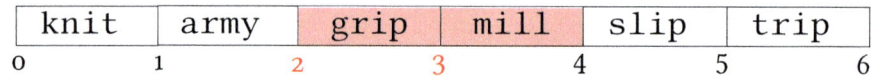

- We look at elements at indices 0 and 1, and compare knit with army.
  Outcome: knit ≥ army, therefore we swap them.
  Current array:

army	knit	grip	mill	slip	trip
0	1	2	3	4	5	6

Exercises in Sorting and Searching

- We look at elements at indices 1 and 2, and compare `knit` with `grip`.
  Outcome: `knit` ≥ `grip`, therefore we swap them.
  Current array:

army	grip	knit	mill	slip	trip	
0	1	2	3	4	5	6

- We look at elements at indices 2 and 3, and compare `knit` with `mill`.
  Outcome: `knit` ≤ `mill`, therefore no swap is needed.

- We look at elements at indices 3 and 4, and compare `mill` with `slip`.
  Outcome: `mill` ≤ `slip`, therefore no swap is needed.

- We look at elements at indices 4 and 5, and compare `slip` with `trip`.
  Outcome: `slip` ≤ `trip`, therefore no swap is needed.

In this pass, a swap was performed, so we have to do another pass.

Pass number 5

The array currently looks like this:

army	grip	knit	mill	slip	trip	
0	1	2	3	4	5	6

- We look at elements at indices 0 and 1, and compare `army` with `grip`.
  Outcome: `army` ≤ `grip`, therefore no swap is needed.

- We look at elements at indices 1 and 2, and compare `grip` with `knit`.
  Outcome: `grip` ≤ `knit`, therefore no swap is needed.

- We look at elements at indices 2 and 3, and compare `knit` with `mill`.
  Outcome: `knit` ≤ `mill`, therefore no swap is needed.

- We look at elements at indices 3 and 4, and compare `mill` with `slip`.
  Outcome: `mill` ≤ `slip`, therefore no swap is needed.

- We look at elements at indices 4 and 5, and compare `slip` with `trip`.
  Outcome: `slip` ≤ `trip`, therefore no swap is needed.

No swaps were performed in this pass, so we are done.
Final array:

army	grip	knit	mill	slip	trip	
0	1	2	3	4	5	6

2.6 Worked Example 6: Sorting a five element array (in four passes)

We start with the input array:

pawn	bird	heat	soil	crew
0	1	2	3	4

and want to sort it using bubblesort.

Pass number 1

The array currently looks like this:

pawn	bird	heat	soil	crew
0	1	2	3	4

- We look at elements at indices 0 and 1, and compare pawn with bird.
  Outcome: pawn ≥ bird, therefore we swap them.
  Current array:

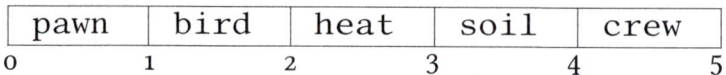

- We look at elements at indices 1 and 2, and compare pawn with heat.
  Outcome: pawn ≥ heat, therefore we swap them.
  Current array:

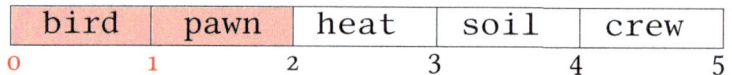

- We look at elements at indices 2 and 3, and compare pawn with soil.
  Outcome: pawn ≤ soil, therefore no swap is needed.

- We look at elements at indices 3 and 4, and compare soil with crew.
  Outcome: soil ≥ crew, therefore we swap them.
  Current array:

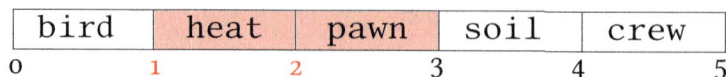

In this pass, a swap was performed, so we have to do another pass.

Pass number 2

The array currently looks like this:

bird	heat	pawn	crew	soil	
0	1	2	3	4	5

- We look at elements at indices 0 and 1, and compare bird with heat.
  Outcome: bird $\leq$ heat, therefore no swap is needed.

- We look at elements at indices 1 and 2, and compare heat with pawn.
  Outcome: heat $\leq$ pawn, therefore no swap is needed.

- We look at elements at indices 2 and 3, and compare pawn with crew.
  Outcome: pawn $\geq$ crew, therefore we swap them.
  Current array:

bird	heat	crew	pawn	soil	
0	1	2	3	4	5

- We look at elements at indices 3 and 4, and compare pawn with soil.
  Outcome: pawn $\leq$ soil, therefore no swap is needed.

In this pass, a swap was performed, so we have to do another pass.

Pass number 3

The array currently looks like this:

bird	heat	crew	pawn	soil	
0	1	2	3	4	5

- We look at elements at indices 0 and 1, and compare bird with heat.
  Outcome: bird $\leq$ heat, therefore no swap is needed.

- We look at elements at indices 1 and 2, and compare heat with crew.
  Outcome: heat $\geq$ crew, therefore we swap them.
  Current array:

bird	crew	heat	pawn	soil	
0	1	2	3	4	5

- We look at elements at indices 2 and 3, and compare heat with pawn.
  Outcome: heat $\leq$ pawn, therefore no swap is needed.

- We look at elements at indices 3 and 4, and compare pawn with soil.
  Outcome: pawn ≤ soil, therefore no swap is needed.

In this pass, a swap was performed, so we have to do another pass.

Pass number 4
The array currently looks like this:

bird	crew	heat	pawn	soil	
0	1	2	3	4	5

- We look at elements at indices 0 and 1, and compare bird with crew.
  Outcome: bird ≤ crew, therefore no swap is needed.

- We look at elements at indices 1 and 2, and compare crew with heat.
  Outcome: crew ≤ heat, therefore no swap is needed.

- We look at elements at indices 2 and 3, and compare heat with pawn.
  Outcome: heat ≤ pawn, therefore no swap is needed.

- We look at elements at indices 3 and 4, and compare pawn with soil.
  Outcome: pawn ≤ soil, therefore no swap is needed.

No swaps were performed in this pass, so we are done.
Final array:

bird	crew	heat	pawn	soil	
0	1	2	3	4	5

Exercises in Sorting and Searching

2.7 Worked Example 7: Sorting a five element array (in three passes)

We start with the input array:

foot	like	view	iron	tube
0	1	2	3	4 5

and want to sort it using bubblesort.

Pass number 1

The array currently looks like this:

foot	like	view	iron	tube
0	1	2	3	4 5

- We look at elements at indices 0 and 1, and compare foot with like.

  Outcome: $foot \leq like$, therefore no swap is needed.

- We look at elements at indices 1 and 2, and compare like with view.

  Outcome: $like \leq view$, therefore no swap is needed.

- We look at elements at indices 2 and 3, and compare view with iron.

  Outcome: $view \geq iron$, therefore we swap them.

  Current array:

  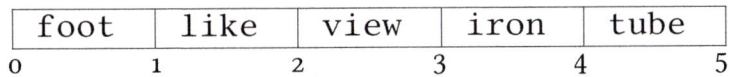

- We look at elements at indices 3 and 4, and compare view with tube.

  Outcome: $view \geq tube$, therefore we swap them.

  Current array:

foot	like	iron	tube	view
0	1	2	3	4 5

In this pass, a swap was performed, so we have to do another pass.

Pass number 2

The array currently looks like this:

foot	like	iron	tube	view	
0	1	2	3	4	5

- We look at elements at indices 0 and 1, and compare foot with like.
  Outcome: foot $\leq$ like, therefore no swap is needed.

- We look at elements at indices 1 and 2, and compare like with iron.
  Outcome: like $\geq$ iron, therefore we swap them.
  Current array:

foot	iron	like	tube	view	
0	1	2	3	4	5

- We look at elements at indices 2 and 3, and compare like with tube.
  Outcome: like $\leq$ tube, therefore no swap is needed.

- We look at elements at indices 3 and 4, and compare tube with view.
  Outcome: tube $\leq$ view, therefore no swap is needed.

In this pass, a swap was performed, so we have to do another pass.

Pass number 3

The array currently looks like this:

foot	iron	like	tube	view	
0	1	2	3	4	5

- We look at elements at indices 0 and 1, and compare foot with iron.
  Outcome: foot $\leq$ iron, therefore no swap is needed.

- We look at elements at indices 1 and 2, and compare iron with like.
  Outcome: iron $\leq$ like, therefore no swap is needed.

- We look at elements at indices 2 and 3, and compare like with tube.
  Outcome: like $\leq$ tube, therefore no swap is needed.

- We look at elements at indices 3 and 4, and compare tube with view.
  Outcome: tube $\leq$ view, therefore no swap is needed.

No swaps were performed in this pass, so we are done.
Final array:

foot	iron	like	tube	view
0	1	2	3	4	5

2.8 Worked Example 8: Sorting a seven element array (in five passes)

We start with the input array:

lamp	dorm	bird	unit	bike	easy	young
0	1	2	3	4	5	6	7

and want to sort it using bubblesort.

Pass number 1

The array currently looks like this:

lamp	dorm	bird	unit	bike	easy	young
0	1	2	3	4	5	6	7

- We look at elements at indices 0 and 1, and compare lamp with dorm.

  Outcome: lamp $\geq$ dorm, therefore we swap them.

  Current array:

dorm	lamp	bird	unit	bike	easy	young
0	1	2	3	4	5	6	7

- We look at elements at indices 1 and 2, and compare lamp with bird.

  Outcome: lamp $\geq$ bird, therefore we swap them.

  Current array:

dorm	bird	lamp	unit	bike	easy	young
0	1	2	3	4	5	6	7

- We look at elements at indices 2 and 3, and compare lamp with unit.

  Outcome: lamp $\leq$ unit, therefore no swap is needed.

- We look at elements at indices 3 and 4, and compare unit with bike.

  Outcome: unit $\geq$ bike, therefore we swap them.

  Current array:

dorm	bird	lamp	bike	unit	easy	young
0	1	2	3	4	5	6	7

- We look at elements at indices 4 and 5, and compare unit with easy.

  Outcome: unit ≥ easy, therefore we swap them.

  Current array:

dorm	bird	lamp	bike	easy	unit	young	
0	1	2	3	4	5	6	7

- We look at elements at indices 5 and 6, and compare unit with young.

  Outcome: unit ≤ young, therefore no swap is needed.

In this pass, a swap was performed, so we have to do another pass.

Pass number 2

The array currently looks like this:

dorm	bird	lamp	bike	easy	unit	young	
0	1	2	3	4	5	6	7

- We look at elements at indices 0 and 1, and compare dorm with bird.

  Outcome: dorm ≥ bird, therefore we swap them.

  Current array:

bird	dorm	lamp	bike	easy	unit	young	
0	1	2	3	4	5	6	7

- We look at elements at indices 1 and 2, and compare dorm with lamp.

  Outcome: dorm ≤ lamp, therefore no swap is needed.

- We look at elements at indices 2 and 3, and compare lamp with bike.

  Outcome: lamp ≥ bike, therefore we swap them.

  Current array:

bird	dorm	bike	lamp	easy	unit	young	
0	1	2	3	4	5	6	7

- We look at elements at indices 3 and 4, and compare lamp with easy.

  Outcome: lamp ≥ easy, therefore we swap them.

  Current array:

bird	dorm	bike	easy	lamp	unit	young	
0	1	2	3	4	5	6	7

- We look at elements at indices 4 and 5, and compare `lamp` with `unit`.
  Outcome: $lamp \leq unit$, therefore no swap is needed.

- We look at elements at indices 5 and 6, and compare `unit` with `young`.
  Outcome: $unit \leq young$, therefore no swap is needed.

In this pass, a swap was performed, so we have to do another pass.

Pass number 3

The array currently looks like this:

bird	dorm	bike	easy	lamp	unit	young
0	1	2	3	4	5	6	7

- We look at elements at indices 0 and 1, and compare `bird` with `dorm`.
  Outcome: $bird \leq dorm$, therefore no swap is needed.

- We look at elements at indices 1 and 2, and compare `dorm` with `bike`.
  Outcome: $dorm \geq bike$, therefore we swap them.
  Current array:

bird	bike	dorm	easy	lamp	unit	young
0	1	2	3	4	5	6	7

- We look at elements at indices 2 and 3, and compare `dorm` with `easy`.
  Outcome: $dorm \leq easy$, therefore no swap is needed.

- We look at elements at indices 3 and 4, and compare `easy` with `lamp`.
  Outcome: $easy \leq lamp$, therefore no swap is needed.

- We look at elements at indices 4 and 5, and compare `lamp` with `unit`.
  Outcome: $lamp \leq unit$, therefore no swap is needed.

- We look at elements at indices 5 and 6, and compare `unit` with `young`.
  Outcome: $unit \leq young$, therefore no swap is needed.

In this pass, a swap was performed, so we have to do another pass.

Exercises in Sorting and Searching

Pass number 4
The array currently looks like this:

bird	bike	dorm	easy	lamp	unit	young
0	1	2	3	4	5	6	7

- We look at elements at indices 0 and 1, and compare bird with bike.
  Outcome: bird $\geq$ bike, therefore we swap them.
  Current array:

bike	bird	dorm	easy	lamp	unit	young
0	1	2	3	4	5	6	7

- We look at elements at indices 1 and 2, and compare bird with dorm.
  Outcome: bird $\leq$ dorm, therefore no swap is needed.

- We look at elements at indices 2 and 3, and compare dorm with easy.
  Outcome: dorm $\leq$ easy, therefore no swap is needed.

- We look at elements at indices 3 and 4, and compare easy with lamp.
  Outcome: easy $\leq$ lamp, therefore no swap is needed.

- We look at elements at indices 4 and 5, and compare lamp with unit.
  Outcome: lamp $\leq$ unit, therefore no swap is needed.

- We look at elements at indices 5 and 6, and compare unit with young.
  Outcome: unit $\leq$ young, therefore no swap is needed.

In this pass, a swap was performed, so we have to do another pass.

Pass number 5
The array currently looks like this:

bike	bird	dorm	easy	lamp	unit	young
0	1	2	3	4	5	6	7

- We look at elements at indices 0 and 1, and compare bike with bird.
  Outcome: bike $\leq$ bird, therefore no swap is needed.

- We look at elements at indices 1 and 2, and compare bird with dorm.
  Outcome: bird $\leq$ dorm, therefore no swap is needed.

- We look at elements at indices 2 and 3, and compare dorm with easy.
  Outcome: dorm ≤ easy, therefore no swap is needed.

- We look at elements at indices 3 and 4, and compare easy with lamp.
  Outcome: easy ≤ lamp, therefore no swap is needed.

- We look at elements at indices 4 and 5, and compare lamp with unit.
  Outcome: lamp ≤ unit, therefore no swap is needed.

- We look at elements at indices 5 and 6, and compare unit with young.
  Outcome: unit ≤ young, therefore no swap is needed.

No swaps were performed in this pass, so we are done.
Final array:

bike	bird	dorm	easy	lamp	unit	young
0	1	2	3	4	5	6	7

Chapter 3
Mergesort

3.1 Worked Example 1: Sorting a four element array

We start with the following array

view	loop	bird	youth
0	1	2	3	4

and want to sort it using mergesort.

Pass 1 of merging

We currently have the following set of sublists:

view
0	1

loop
0	1

bird
0	1

youth
0	1

We now merge the 1st and 2nd sublists together

- We are currently merging [view] with [loop]. Comparing view with loop, we find that: loop ≤ view, so we append loop onto the merged list.

  Merged list so far:

  $$[\text{loop}]$$

We got to the end of 2nd list, so now we just add in all the remaining elements of the 1st list
Result of merging:

$$[\text{loop}, \text{view}]$$

We now merge the 3rd and 4th sublists together

- We are currently merging [bird] with [youth]. Comparing bird with youth, we find that:

  bird ≤ youth, so we append bird onto the merged list.

  Merged list so far:

$$[\text{bird}]$$

We got to the end of 1st list, so just add in all the remaining elements of the 2nd list
Result of merging:

$$[\text{bird}, \text{youth}]$$

Pass 2 of merging

We currently have the following set of sublists:

loop	view
0	1	2

bird	youth
0	1	2

We now merge the 1st and 2nd sublists together

- We are currently merging [loop, view] with [bird, youth]. Comparing loop with bird, we find that:

  bird ≤ loop, so we append bird onto the merged list.

  Merged list so far:

$$[\text{bird}]$$

- We are currently merging [loop, view] with [~~bird~~, youth]. Comparing loop with youth, we find that:

  loop ≤ youth, so we append loop onto the merged list.

  Merged list so far:

Exercises in Sorting and Searching

[bird, loop]

- We are currently merging [~~loop~~, view] with [~~bird~~, youth]. Comparing view with youth, we find that:

  view ≤ youth, so we append view onto the merged list.

  Merged list so far:

  [bird, loop, view]

We got to the end of 1st list, so just add in all the remaining elements of the 2nd list
Result of merging:

[bird, loop, view, youth]

The final result of mergesort is:

bird	loop	view	youth
0	1	2	3	4

3.2 Worked Example 2: Sorting a four element array

We start with the following array

tube	queue	weed	note
0	1	2	3	4

and want to sort it using mergesort.

Pass 1 of merging

We currently have the following set of sublists:

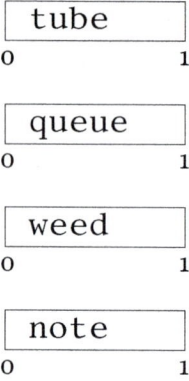

We now merge the 1st and 2nd sublists together

- We are currently merging [tube] with [queue]. Comparing tube with queue, we find that:

  queue ≤ tube, so we append queue onto the merged list.

  Merged list so far:

  [queue]

We got to the end of 2nd list, so now we just add in all the remaining elements of the 1st list
Result of merging:

[queue, tube]

We now merge the 3rd and 4th sublists together

- We are currently merging [weed] with [note]. Comparing weed with note, we find that:

  note ≤ weed, so we append note onto the merged list.

  Merged list so far:

Exercises in Sorting and Searching

[note]

We got to the end of 2nd list, so now we just add in all the remaining elements of the 1st list
Result of merging:

[note, weed]

Pass 2 of merging

We currently have the following set of sublists:

queue	tube
0	1	2

note	weed
0	1	2

We now merge the 1st and 2nd sublists together

- We are currently merging [queue, tube] with [note, weed]. Comparing queue with note, we find that:

  note ≤ queue, so we append note onto the merged list.

  Merged list so far:

  [note]

- We are currently merging [queue, tube] with [note, weed]. Comparing queue with weed, we find that:

  queue ≤ weed, so we append queue onto the merged list.

  Merged list so far:

  [note, queue]

- We are currently merging [queue, tube] with [note, weed]. Comparing tube with weed, we find that:

  tube ≤ weed, so we append tube onto the merged list.

  Merged list so far:

  [note, queue, tube]

We got to the end of 1st list, so just add in all the remaining elements of the 2nd list
Result of merging:

[note, queue, tube, weed]

The final result of mergesort is:

note	queue	tube	weed
0   1   2   3   4

Exercises in Sorting and Searching

3.3 Worked Example 3: Sorting a six element array

We start with the following array

note	item	norm	mine	army	fund
0	1	2	3	4	5	6

and want to sort it using mergesort.

Pass 1 of merging

We currently have the following set of sublists:

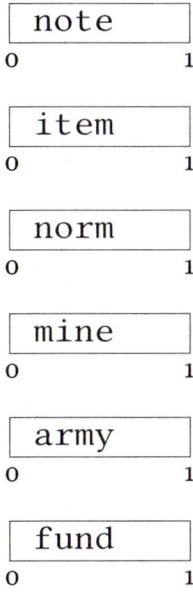

We now merge the 1st and 2nd sublists together

- We are currently merging [note] with [item]. Comparing note with item, we find that: item ≤ note, so we append item onto the merged list.
  Merged list so far:

  [item]

We got to the end of 2nd list, so now we just add in all the remaining elements of the 1st list
Result of merging:

[item, note]

We now merge the 3rd and 4th sublists together

- We are currently merging [norm] with [mine]. Comparing norm with mine, we find that: mine ≤ norm, so we append mine onto the merged list.

  Merged list so far:

  $$[\text{mine}]$$

We got to the end of 2nd list, so now we just add in all the remaining elements of the 1st list
Result of merging:

$$[\text{mine}, \text{norm}]$$

We now merge the 5th and 6th sublists together

- We are currently merging [army] with [fund]. Comparing army with fund, we find that: army ≤ fund, so we append army onto the merged list.

  Merged list so far:

  $$[\text{army}]$$

We got to the end of 1st list, so just add in all the remaining elements of the 2nd list
Result of merging:

$$[\text{army}, \text{fund}]$$

Pass 2 of merging

We currently have the following set of sublists:

item	note
0	1	2

mine	norm
0	1	2

army	fund
0	1	2

We now merge the 1st and 2nd sublists together

- We are currently merging [item, note] with [mine, norm]. Comparing item with mine, we find that: item ≤ mine, so we append item onto the merged list.

  Merged list so far:

$$[\text{item}]$$

- We are currently merging [i̶t̶e̶m̶, note] with [mine, norm]. Comparing note with mine, we find that:

  mine ≤ note, so we append mine onto the merged list.

  Merged list so far:

  $$[\text{item}, \text{mine}]$$

- We are currently merging [i̶t̶e̶m̶, note] with [m̶i̶n̶e̶, norm]. Comparing note with norm, we find that:

  norm ≤ note, so we append norm onto the merged list.

  Merged list so far:

  $$[\text{item}, \text{mine}, \text{norm}]$$

We got to the end of 2nd list, so now we just add in all the remaining elements of the 1st list
Result of merging:

$$[\text{item}, \text{mine}, \text{norm}, \text{note}]$$

Pass 3 of merging

We currently have the following set of sublists:

item	mine	norm	note
0	1	2	3	4

army	fund
0	1	2

We now merge the 1st and 2nd sublists together

- We are currently merging [item, mine, norm, note] with [army, fund]. Comparing item with army, we find that:

  army ≤ item, so we append army onto the merged list.

  Merged list so far:

  $$[\text{army}]$$

- We are currently merging [`item`, `mine`, `norm`, `note`] with [~~`army`~~, `fund`]. Comparing `item` with `fund`, we find that:

    `fund` $\leq$ `item`, so we append `fund` onto the merged list.

    Merged list so far:

    $$[\text{army}, \text{fund}]$$

We got to the end of 2nd list, so now we just add in all the remaining elements of the 1st list
Result of merging:

$$[\text{army}, \text{fund}, \text{item}, \text{mine}, \text{norm}, \text{note}]$$

The final result of mergesort is:

army	fund	item	mine	norm	note
0	1	2	3	4	5	6

Exercises in Sorting and Searching

3.4 Worked Example 4: Sorting an array with six elements

We start with the following array

fund	slab	riot	edge	item	quit
0	1	2	3	4	5	6

and want to sort it using mergesort.

Pass 1 of merging

We currently have the following set of sublists:

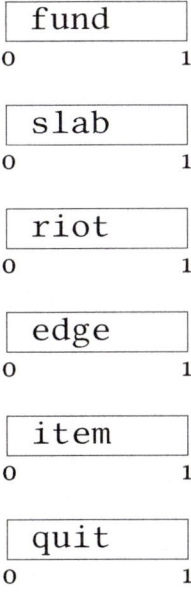

We now merge the 1st and 2nd sublists together

- We are currently merging [fund] with [slab]. Comparing fund with slab, we find that: fund ≤ slab, so we append fund onto the merged list.
  Merged list so far:

  [fund]

We got to the end of 1st list, so just add in all the remaining elements of the 2nd list
Result of merging:

[fund, slab]

We now merge the 3rd and 4th sublists together

- We are currently merging [riot] with [edge]. Comparing riot with edge, we find that: edge ≤ riot, so we append edge onto the merged list.

  Merged list so far:

  $$[\text{edge}]$$

We got to the end of 2nd list, so now we just add in all the remaining elements of the 1st list
Result of merging:

$$[\text{edge}, \text{riot}]$$

We now merge the 5th and 6th sublists together

- We are currently merging [item] with [quit]. Comparing item with quit, we find that: item ≤ quit, so we append item onto the merged list.

  Merged list so far:

  $$[\text{item}]$$

We got to the end of 1st list, so just add in all the remaining elements of the 2nd list
Result of merging:

$$[\text{item}, \text{quit}]$$

Pass 2 of merging

We currently have the following set of sublists:

fund	slab
0	1	2

edge	riot
0	1	2

item	quit
0	1	2

We now merge the 1st and 2nd sublists together

- We are currently merging [fund, slab] with [edge, riot]. Comparing fund with edge, we find that:

  edge ≤ fund, so we append edge onto the merged list.

  Merged list so far:

Exercises in Sorting and Searching

$$[\text{edge}]$$

- We are currently merging [fund, slab] with [edge, riot]. Comparing fund with riot, we find that:

  fund ≤ riot, so we append fund onto the merged list.

  Merged list so far:

  $$[\text{edge, fund}]$$

- We are currently merging [~~fund~~, slab] with [~~edge~~, riot]. Comparing slab with riot, we find that:

  riot ≤ slab, so we append riot onto the merged list.

  Merged list so far:

  $$[\text{edge, fund, riot}]$$

We got to the end of 2nd list, so now we just add in all the remaining elements of the 1st list
Result of merging:

$$[\text{edge, fund, riot, slab}]$$

Pass 3 of merging

We currently have the following set of sublists:

edge	fund	riot	slab
0	1	2	3	4

item	quit
0	1	2

We now merge the 1st and 2nd sublists together

- We are currently merging [edge, fund, riot, slab] with [item, quit]. Comparing edge with item, we find that:

  edge ≤ item, so we append edge onto the merged list.

  Merged list so far:

  $$[\text{edge}]$$

- We are currently merging [~~edge~~, fund, riot, slab] with [item, quit]. Comparing fund with item, we find that:

  fund ≤ item, so we append fund onto the merged list.

  Merged list so far:

  $$[\text{edge}, \text{fund}]$$

- We are currently merging [~~edge~~, ~~fund~~, riot, slab] with [item, quit]. Comparing riot with item, we find that:

  item ≤ riot, so we append item onto the merged list.

  Merged list so far:

  $$[\text{edge}, \text{fund}, \text{item}]$$

- We are currently merging [~~edge~~, ~~fund~~, riot, slab] with [~~item~~, quit]. Comparing riot with quit, we find that:

  quit ≤ riot, so we append quit onto the merged list.

  Merged list so far:

  $$[\text{edge}, \text{fund}, \text{item}, \text{quit}]$$

We got to the end of 2nd list, so now we just add in all the remaining elements of the 1st list

Result of merging:

$$[\text{edge}, \text{fund}, \text{item}, \text{quit}, \text{riot}, \text{slab}]$$

The final result of mergesort is:

edge	fund	item	quit	riot	slab
0	1	2	3	4	5	6

Exercises in Sorting and Searching

3.5 Worked Example 5: Sorting an array with six elements

We start with the following array

year	golf	young	neck	mill	slip
0	1	2	3	4	5	6

and want to sort it using mergesort.

Pass 1 of merging

We currently have the following set of sublists:

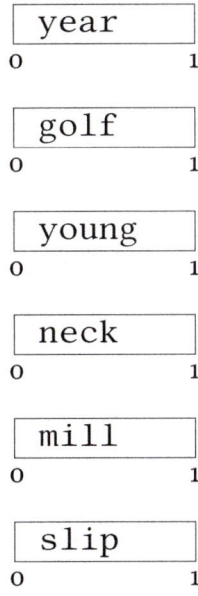

We now merge the 1st and 2nd sublists together

- We are currently merging [year] with [golf]. Comparing year with golf, we find that: golf ≤ year, so we append golf onto the merged list.
  Merged list so far:

$$[golf]$$

We got to the end of 2nd list, so now we just add in all the remaining elements of the 1st list
Result of merging:

$$[golf, year]$$

We now merge the 3rd and 4th sublists together

- We are currently merging [young] with [neck]. Comparing young with neck, we find that:

  neck ≤ young, so we append neck onto the merged list.

  Merged list so far:

  $$[\text{neck}]$$

We got to the end of 2nd list, so now we just add in all the remaining elements of the 1st list
Result of merging:

$$[\text{neck}, \text{young}]$$

We now merge the 5th and 6th sublists together

- We are currently merging [mill] with [slip]. Comparing mill with slip, we find that:

  mill ≤ slip, so we append mill onto the merged list.

  Merged list so far:

  $$[\text{mill}]$$

We got to the end of 1st list, so just add in all the remaining elements of the 2nd list
Result of merging:

$$[\text{mill}, \text{slip}]$$

Pass 2 of merging

We currently have the following set of sublists:

golf	year
0	1	2

neck	young
0	1	2

mill	slip
0	1	2

We now merge the 1st and 2nd sublists together

- We are currently merging [golf, year] with [neck, young]. Comparing golf with neck, we find that:

  golf ≤ neck, so we append golf onto the merged list.

  Merged list so far:

$$[\text{golf}]$$

- We are currently merging [~~golf~~, year] with [neck, young]. Comparing year with neck, we find that:

  neck ≤ year, so we append neck onto the merged list.

  Merged list so far:

  $$[\text{golf}, \text{neck}]$$

- We are currently merging [~~golf~~, year] with [~~neck~~, young]. Comparing year with young, we find that:

  year ≤ young, so we append year onto the merged list.

  Merged list so far:

  $$[\text{golf}, \text{neck}, \text{year}]$$

We got to the end of 1st list, so just add in all the remaining elements of the 2nd list
Result of merging:

$$[\text{golf}, \text{neck}, \text{year}, \text{young}]$$

Pass 3 of merging

We currently have the following set of sublists:

golf	neck	year	young
0	1	2	3	4

mill	slip
0	1	2

We now merge the 1st and 2nd sublists together

- We are currently merging [golf, neck, year, young] with [mill, slip]. Comparing golf with mill, we find that:

  golf ≤ mill, so we append golf onto the merged list.

  Merged list so far:

  $$[\text{golf}]$$

- We are currently merging [~~golf~~, neck, year, young] with [mill, slip]. Comparing neck with mill, we find that:

  mill ≤ neck, so we append mill onto the merged list.

  Merged list so far:

  $$[\texttt{golf}, \texttt{mill}]$$

- We are currently merging [~~golf~~, neck, year, young] with [~~mill~~, slip]. Comparing neck with slip, we find that:

  neck ≤ slip, so we append neck onto the merged list.

  Merged list so far:

  $$[\texttt{golf}, \texttt{mill}, \texttt{neck}]$$

- We are currently merging [~~golf~~, ~~neck~~, year, young] with [~~mill~~, slip]. Comparing year with slip, we find that:

  slip ≤ year, so we append slip onto the merged list.

  Merged list so far:

  $$[\texttt{golf}, \texttt{mill}, \texttt{neck}, \texttt{slip}]$$

We got to the end of 2nd list, so now we just add in all the remaining elements of the 1st list
Result of merging:

$$[\texttt{golf}, \texttt{mill}, \texttt{neck}, \texttt{slip}, \texttt{year}, \texttt{young}]$$

The final result of mergesort is:

golf	mill	neck	slip	year	young
0	1	2	3	4	5	6

Exercises in Sorting and Searching

3.6 Worked Example 6: Sorting an array with five elements

We start with the following array

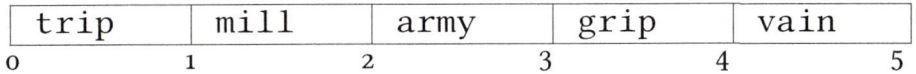

and want to sort it using mergesort.

Pass 1 of merging

We currently have the following set of sublists:

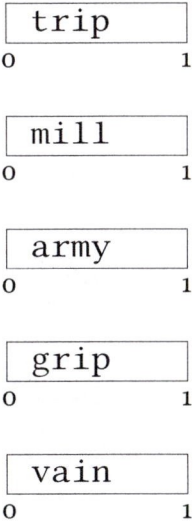

We now merge the 1st and 2nd sublists together

- We are currently merging [trip] with [mill]. Comparing trip with mill, we find that: mill ≤ trip, so we append mill onto the merged list.
  Merged list so far:

  [mill]

We got to the end of 2nd list, so now we just add in all the remaining elements of the 1st list
Result of merging:

[mill, trip]

We now merge the 3rd and 4th sublists together

- We are currently merging [army] with [grip]. Comparing army with grip, we find that:

    army ≤ grip, so we append army onto the merged list.

    Merged list so far:

    $$[\text{army}]$$

We got to the end of 1st list, so just add in all the remaining elements of the 2nd list
Result of merging:

$$[\text{army}, \text{grip}]$$

Pass 2 of merging

We currently have the following set of sublists:

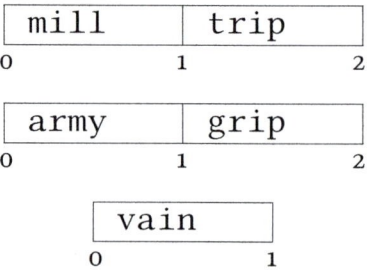

We now merge the 1st and 2nd sublists together

- We are currently merging [mill, trip] with [army, grip]. Comparing mill with army, we find that:

    army ≤ mill, so we append army onto the merged list.

    Merged list so far:

    $$[\text{army}]$$

- We are currently merging [mill, trip] with [~~army~~, grip]. Comparing mill with grip, we find that:

    grip ≤ mill, so we append grip onto the merged list.

    Merged list so far:

    $$[\text{army}, \text{grip}]$$

We got to the end of 2nd list, so now we just add in all the remaining elements of the 1st list
Result of merging:

$$[\text{army}, \text{grip}, \text{mill}, \text{trip}]$$

Pass 3 of merging

We currently have the following set of sublists:

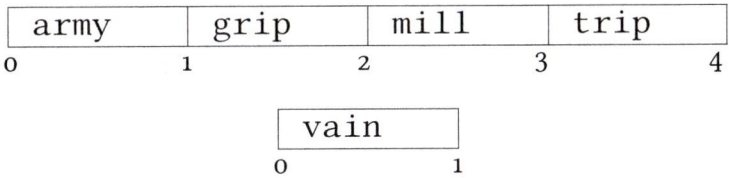

We now merge the 1st and 2nd sublists together

- We are currently merging [army, grip, mill, trip] with [vain]. Comparing army with vain, we find that:

  army ≤ vain, so we append army onto the merged list.

  Merged list so far:

  $$[army]$$

- We are currently merging [~~army~~, grip, mill, trip] with [vain]. Comparing grip with vain, we find that:

  grip ≤ vain, so we append grip onto the merged list.

  Merged list so far:

  $$[army, grip]$$

- We are currently merging [~~army~~, ~~grip~~, mill, trip] with [vain]. Comparing mill with vain, we find that:

  mill ≤ vain, so we append mill onto the merged list.

  Merged list so far:

  $$[army, grip, mill]$$

- We are currently merging [~~army~~, ~~grip~~, ~~mill~~, trip] with [vain]. Comparing trip with vain, we find that:

  trip ≤ vain, so we append trip onto the merged list.

  Merged list so far:

  $$[army, grip, mill, trip]$$

We got to the end of 1st list, so just add in all the remaining elements of the 2nd list
Result of merging:

[army, grip, mill, trip, vain]

The final result of mergesort is:

army	grip	mill	trip	vain
0	1	2	3	4	5

| *Exercises in Sorting and Searching*

3.7 Worked Example 7: Sorting an array with four elements

We start with the following array

pawn	bird	heat	soil
0	1	2	3	4

and want to sort it using mergesort.

Pass 1 of merging

We currently have the following set of sublists:

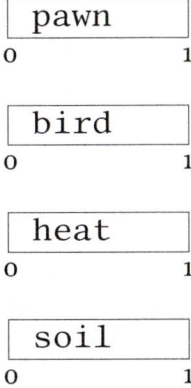

We now merge the 1st and 2nd sublists together

- We are currently merging [pawn] with [bird]. Comparing pawn with bird, we find that: bird ≤ pawn, so we append bird onto the merged list.

  Merged list so far:

  $$[\text{bird}]$$

We got to the end of 2nd list, so now we just add in all the remaining elements of the 1st list
Result of merging:

$$[\text{bird, pawn}]$$

We now merge the 3rd and 4th sublists together

- We are currently merging [heat] with [soil]. Comparing heat with soil, we find that: heat ≤ soil, so we append heat onto the merged list.

  Merged list so far:

$$[\text{heat}]$$

We got to the end of 1st list, so just add in all the remaining elements of the 2nd list
Result of merging:

$$[\text{heat}, \text{soil}]$$

Pass 2 of merging

We currently have the following set of sublists:

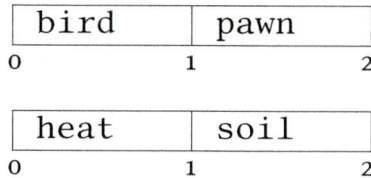

We now merge the 1st and 2nd sublists together

- We are currently merging [bird, pawn] with [heat, soil]. Comparing bird with heat, we find that:

    bird $\leq$ heat, so we append bird onto the merged list.

    Merged list so far:

    $$[\text{bird}]$$

- We are currently merging [~~bird~~, pawn] with [heat, soil]. Comparing pawn with heat, we find that:

    heat $\leq$ pawn, so we append heat onto the merged list.

    Merged list so far:

    $$[\text{bird}, \text{heat}]$$

- We are currently merging [~~bird~~, pawn] with [~~heat~~, soil]. Comparing pawn with soil, we find that:

    pawn $\leq$ soil, so we append pawn onto the merged list.

    Merged list so far:

    $$[\text{bird}, \text{heat}, \text{pawn}]$$

We got to the end of 1st list, so just add in all the remaining elements of the 2nd list
Result of merging:

[bird, heat, pawn, soil]

The final result of mergesort is:

bird	heat	pawn	soil
0	1	2	3	4

3.8 Worked Example 8: Sorting an array with four elements

We start with the following array

bold	foot	like	view
0	1	2	3	4

and want to sort it using mergesort.

Pass 1 of merging

We currently have the following set of sublists:

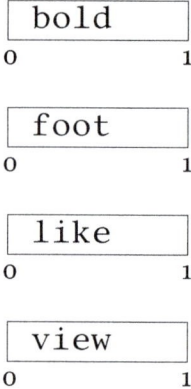

We now merge the 1st and 2nd sublists together

- We are currently merging [bold] with [foot]. Comparing bold with foot, we find that: bold ≤ foot, so we append bold onto the merged list.
  Merged list so far:

  [bold]

We got to the end of 1st list, so just add in all the remaining elements of the 2nd list
Result of merging:

[bold, foot]

We now merge the 3rd and 4th sublists together

- We are currently merging [like] with [view]. Comparing like with view, we find that: like ≤ view, so we append like onto the merged list.
  Merged list so far:

Exercises in Sorting and Searching

$$[\text{like}]$$

We got to the end of 1st list, so just add in all the remaining elements of the 2nd list
Result of merging:

$$[\text{like}, \text{view}]$$

Pass 2 of merging

We currently have the following set of sublists:

bold	foot
0	1	2

like	view
0	1	2

We now merge the 1st and 2nd sublists together

- We are currently merging [bold, foot] with [like, view]. Comparing bold with like, we find that:

  bold ≤ like, so we append bold onto the merged list.

  Merged list so far:

  $$[\text{bold}]$$

- We are currently merging [~~bold~~, foot] with [like, view]. Comparing foot with like, we find that:

  foot ≤ like, so we append foot onto the merged list.

  Merged list so far:

  $$[\text{bold}, \text{foot}]$$

We got to the end of 1st list, so just add in all the remaining elements of the 2nd list
Result of merging:

$$[\text{bold}, \text{foot}, \text{like}, \text{view}]$$

The final result of mergesort is:

bold	foot	like	view
0	1	2	3	4

Part II

SEARCHING ALGORITHMS

Chapter 4
Linear search

4.1 Worked Example 1: Present in middle of input array

We are given the following array

youth	view	loop	tube	bird
0	1	2	3	4	5

and we want to find whether `view` is present in the array.

- Current index = 0

youth	view	loop	tube	bird
0	1	2	3	4	5

Is `youth` the word we are looking for? No, therefore we look at the next element of the array.

- Current index = 1

youth	view	loop	tube	bird
0	1	2	3	4	5

Is `view` the word we are looking for? Yes, we've found `view` at index 1 in the list.

4.2 Worked Example 2: Not present in input array

We are given the following array

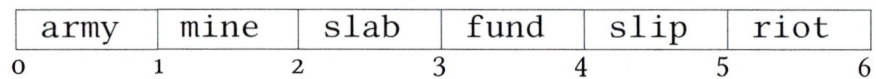

and we want to find whether `norm` is present in the array.

- Current index = 0

| army | mine | slab | fund | slip | riot |
| 0 | 1 | 2 | 3 | 4 | 5 | 6 |

Is `army` the word we are looking for? No, therefore we look at the next element of the array.

- Current index = 1

| army | mine | slab | fund | slip | riot |
| 0 | 1 | 2 | 3 | 4 | 5 | 6 |

Is `mine` the word we are looking for? No, therefore we look at the next element of the array.

- Current index = 2

| army | mine | slab | fund | slip | riot |
| 0 | 1 | 2 | 3 | 4 | 5 | 6 |

Is `slab` the word we are looking for? No, therefore we look at the next element of the array.

- Current index = 3

| army | mine | slab | fund | slip | riot |
| 0 | 1 | 2 | 3 | 4 | 5 | 6 |

Is `fund` the word we are looking for? No, therefore we look at the next element of the array.

- Current index = 4

| army | mine | slab | fund | slip | riot |
| 0 | 1 | 2 | 3 | 4 | 5 | 6 |

Is `slip` the word we are looking for? No, therefore we look at the next element of the array.

Exercises in Sorting and Searching

- Current index = 5

army	mine	slab	fund	slip	riot	
0	1	2	3	4	5	6

Is `riot` the word we are looking for? No.

We got to the end of the list and didn't find `norm`. Therefore, it is not in the array.

4.3 Worked Example 3: Present at end of array

We are given the following array

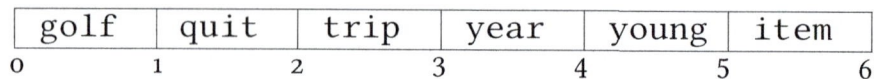

and we want to find whether `item` is present in the array.

- Current index = 0

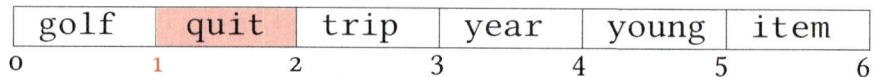

Is `golf` the word we are looking for? No, therefore we look at the next element of the array.

- Current index = 1

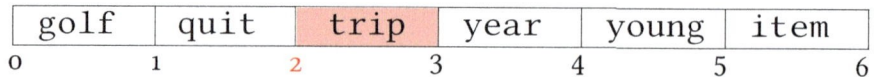

Is `quit` the word we are looking for? No, therefore we look at the next element of the array.

- Current index = 2

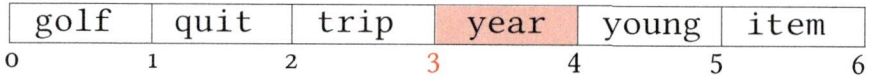

Is `trip` the word we are looking for? No, therefore we look at the next element of the array.

- Current index = 3

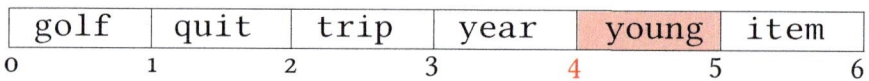

Is `year` the word we are looking for? No, therefore we look at the next element of the array.

- Current index = 4

Is `young` the word we are looking for? No, therefore we look at the next element of the array.

Exercises in Sorting and Searching

- Current index = 5

golf	quit	trip	year	young	item
0	1	2	3	4	5	6

Is `item` the word we are looking for? Yes, we've found `item` at index 5 in the list.

4.4 Worked Example 4: Not present in input array

We are given the following array

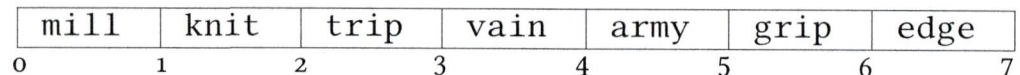

and we want to find whether `slip` is present in the array.

- Current index = 0

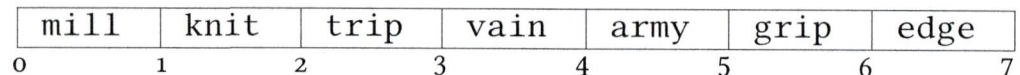

Is `mill` the word we are looking for? No, therefore we look at the next element of the array.

- Current index = 1

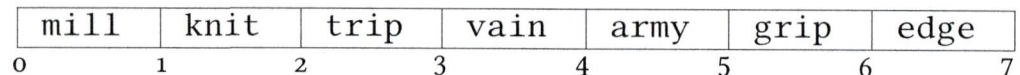

Is `knit` the word we are looking for? No, therefore we look at the next element of the array.

- Current index = 2

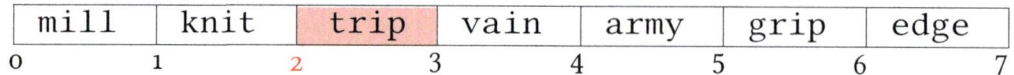

Is `trip` the word we are looking for? No, therefore we look at the next element of the array.

- Current index = 3

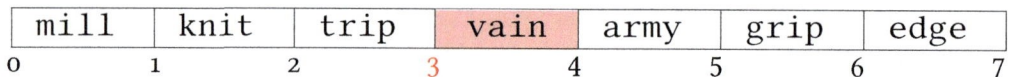

Is `vain` the word we are looking for? No, therefore we look at the next element of the array.

- Current index = 4

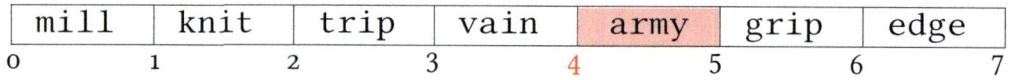

Is `army` the word we are looking for? No, therefore we look at the next element of the array.

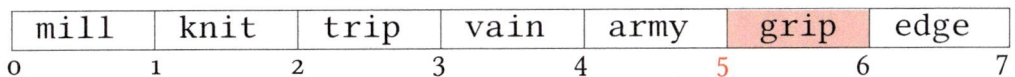

- Current index = 5

mill	knit	trip	vain	army	grip	edge
0	1	2	3	4	5	6	7

Is grip the word we are looking for? No, therefore we look at the next element of the array.

- Current index = 6

mill	knit	trip	vain	army	grip	edge
0	1	2	3	4	5	6	7

Is edge the word we are looking for? No.

We got to the end of the list and didn't find slip. Therefore, it is not in the array.

4.5 Worked Example 5: Present at start of array

We are given the following array

heat	crew	foot	bold	soil	
0	1	2	3	4	5

and we want to find whether heat is present in the array.

- Current index = 0

heat	crew	foot	bold	soil	
0	1	2	3	4	5

Is heat the word we are looking for? Yes, we've found heat at index 0 in the list.

Exercises in Sorting and Searching

4.6 Worked Example 6: Not present in input array

We are given the following array

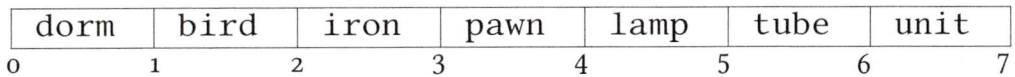

and we want to find whether `view` is present in the array.

- Current index = 0

dorm	bird	iron	pawn	lamp	tube	unit	
0	1	2	3	4	5	6	7

Is `dorm` the word we are looking for? No, therefore we look at the next element of the array.

- Current index = 1

dorm	bird	iron	pawn	lamp	tube	unit	
0	1	2	3	4	5	6	7

Is `bird` the word we are looking for? No, therefore we look at the next element of the array.

- Current index = 2

dorm	bird	iron	pawn	lamp	tube	unit	
0	1	2	3	4	5	6	7

Is `iron` the word we are looking for? No, therefore we look at the next element of the array.

- Current index = 3

dorm	bird	iron	pawn	lamp	tube	unit	
0	1	2	3	4	5	6	7

Is `pawn` the word we are looking for? No, therefore we look at the next element of the array.

- Current index = 4

dorm	bird	iron	pawn	lamp	tube	unit	
0	1	2	3	4	5	6	7

Is `lamp` the word we are looking for? No, therefore we look at the next element of the array.

- Current index = 5

dorm	bird	iron	pawn	lamp	tube	unit	
0	1	2	3	4	5	6	7

Is `tube` the word we are looking for? No, therefore we look at the next element of the array.

- Current index = 6

dorm	bird	iron	pawn	lamp	tube	unit	
0	1	2	3	4	5	6	7

Is `unit` the word we are looking for? No.

We got to the end of the list and didn't find `view`. Therefore, it is not in the array.

Exercises in Sorting and Searching

4.7 Worked Example 7: Present at start of array

We are given the following array

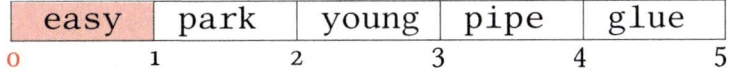

and we want to find whether *easy* is present in the array.

- Current index = 0

easy	park	young	pipe	glue	
0	1	2	3	4	5

Is *easy* the word we are looking for? Yes, we've found *easy* at index 0 in the list.

4.8 Worked Example 8: Not present in input array

We are given the following array

lamp	fund	load	hand	
0	1	2	3	4

and we want to find whether `idea` is present in the array.

- Current index = 0

lamp	fund	load	hand	
0	1	2	3	4

Is lamp the word we are looking for? No, therefore we look at the next element of the array.

- Current index = 1

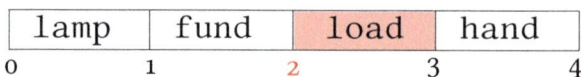

Is fund the word we are looking for? No, therefore we look at the next element of the array.

- Current index = 2

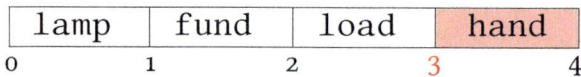

Is load the word we are looking for? No, therefore we look at the next element of the array.

- Current index = 3

lamp	fund	load	hand	
0	1	2	3	4

Is hand the word we are looking for? No.

We got to the end of the list and didn't find `idea`. Therefore, it is not in the array.

Chapter 5
Binary search

5.1 Worked Example 1: Finding an item near the end of the input array

We are given the (sorted) input array:

bird	loop	queue	tube	view	youth
0	1	2	3	4	5	6

and we are trying to find whether `view` is present in the array.

We initialise two variables, `low` and `high` that denote the current range of indices where the query word may be located.

Initially, we set:

- `low` = 0

- `high` = 6

Step 1

Currently, `low` = 0, `high` = 6.

Therefore, we choose as our guess index $\texttt{guess} = (0+6)//2 = 3$ and we compare `tube` with `view`.

`tube` < `view`: therefore we discard the lower half of the current range and middle element.

We update **`low` = 4**.

Now, we have `low` = 4 and `high` = 6.

Step 2

Currently, `low` = 4, `high` = 6.

Therefore, we choose as our guess index $\texttt{guess} = (4+6)//2 = 5$ and we compare `youth` with `view`.

`youth` > `view`. therefore we discard the upper half of the current range and the middle (or 'guess') element.

We do this by setting **`high`** = 5.

Now, we have $\texttt{low} = 4$ and $\texttt{high} = 5$.

Step 3

Currently, $\texttt{low} = 4, \texttt{high} = 5$.

Therefore, we choose as our guess index $\texttt{guess} = (4+5)//2 = 4$ and we compare `view` with `view`.

Note that we have found `view` at index 4, and we are done.

Exercises in Sorting and Searching

5.2 Worked Example 2: Searching for an query not present in the input array

We are given the (sorted) input array:

army	fund	item	mine	norm	note	pace	
0	1	2	3	4	5	6	7

and we are trying to find whether user is present in the array.

We initialise two variables, low and high that denote the current range of indices where the query word may be located.
Initially, we set:

- low = 0
- high = 7

Step 1

Currently, low = 0, high = 7.

Therefore, we choose as our guess index guess = $(0+7)//2 = 3$ and we compare mine with user.

mine $<$ user: therefore we discard the lower half of the current range and middle element.

We update **low = 4**.

Now, we have low = 4 and high = 7.

Step 2

Currently, low = 4, high = 7.

Therefore, we choose as our guess index guess = $(4+7)//2 = 5$ and we compare note with user.

note $<$ user: therefore we discard the lower half of the current range and middle element.

We update **low = 6**.

Now, we have low = 6 and high = 7.

Step 3

Currently, low = 6, high = 7.

Therefore, we choose as our guess index guess = $(6+7)//2 = 6$ and we compare pace with user.

pace $<$ user: therefore we discard the lower half of the current range and middle element.

We update `low` = **7**.

Now, we have $\texttt{low} = 7$ and $\texttt{high} = 7$. We have ended up with an empty range, therefore the query `user` is not present in the original array.

5.3 Worked Example 3: Searching for an element near the start of the input array

We are given the (sorted) input array:

edge	fund	item	quit	riot	slab	trip	year	
0	1	2	3	4	5	6	7	8

and we are trying to find whether fund is present in the array.

We initialise two variables, low and high that denote the current range of indices where the query word may be located.
  Initially, we set:

- low = 0

- high = 8

Step 1

Currently, low = 0, high = 8.

Therefore, we choose as our guess index guess = $(0+8)//2 = 4$ and we compare riot with fund.

riot > fund. therefore we discard the upper half of the current range and the middle (or 'guess') element.

We do this by setting **high** = 4.

Now, we have low = 0 and high = 4.

Step 2

Currently, low = 0, high = 4.

Therefore, we choose as our guess index guess = $(0+4)//2 = 2$ and we compare item with fund.

item > fund. therefore we discard the upper half of the current range and the middle (or 'guess') element.

We do this by setting **high** = 2.

Now, we have low = 0 and high = 2.

Step 3

Currently, low = 0, high = 2.

Therefore, we choose as our guess index guess = $(0+2)//2 = 1$ and we compare fund with fund.

Note that we have found *fund* at index 1, and we are done.

5.4 Worked Example 4: Searching for an element not present in the input array

We are given the (sorted) input array:

army	knit	mill	neck	slip	trip
0	1	2	3	4	5	6

and we are trying to find whether young is present in the array.

We initialise two variables, low and high that denote the current range of indices where the query word may be located.

Initially, we set:

- low = 0

- high = 6

Step 1

Currently, low = 0, high = 6.

Therefore, we choose as our guess index guess = $(0+6)//2 = 3$ and we compare neck with young.

neck < young: therefore we discard the lower half of the current range and middle element.

We update **low = 4**.

Now, we have low = 4 and high = 6.

Step 2

Currently, low = 4, high = 6.

Therefore, we choose as our guess index guess = $(4+6)//2 = 5$ and we compare trip with young.

trip < young: therefore we discard the lower half of the current range and middle element.

We update **low = 6**.

Now, we have low = 6 and high = 6. We have ended up with an empty range, therefore the query young is not present in the original array.

5.5 Worked Example 5: Searching for an element not present in the input array

We are given the (sorted) input array:

bird	edge	heat	pawn	soil	vain
0	1	2	3	4	5	6

and we are trying to find whether `vain` is present in the array.

We initialise two variables, `low` and `high` that denote the current range of indices where the query word may be located.

Initially, we set:

- `low` = 0

- `high` = 6

Step 1

Currently, `low` = 0, `high` = 6.

Therefore, we choose as our guess index $guess = (0+6)//2 = 3$ and we compare `pawn` with `vain`.

`pawn` < `vain`: therefore we discard the lower half of the current range and middle element.

We update **`low` = 4**.

Now, we have `low` = 4 and `high` = 6.

Step 2

Currently, `low` = 4, `high` = 6.

Therefore, we choose as our guess index $guess = (4+6)//2 = 5$ and we compare `vain` with `vain`.

Note that we have found `vain` at index 5, and we are done.

Exercises in Sorting and Searching

5.6 Worked Example 6: Searching for a element not present in the input array

We are given the (sorted) input array:

foot	iron	like	tube	view
0	1	2	3	4	5

and we are trying to find whether `bold` is present in the array.

We initialise two variables, `low` and `high` that denote the current range of indices where the query word may be located.

Initially, we set:

- `low` = 0

- `high` = 5

Step 1

Currently, `low` = 0, `high` = 5.

Therefore, we choose as our guess index $guess = (0+5)//2 = 2$ and we compare `like` with `bold`.

`like` > `bold`. therefore we discard the upper half of the current range and the middle (or 'guess') element.

We do this by setting **high** = 2.

Now, we have `low` = 0 and `high` = 2.

Step 2

Currently, `low` = 0, `high` = 2.

Therefore, we choose as our guess index $guess = (0+2)//2 = 1$ and we compare `iron` with `bold`.

`iron` > `bold`. therefore we discard the upper half of the current range and the middle (or 'guess') element.

We do this by setting **high** = 1.

Now, we have `low` = 0 and `high` = 1.

Step 3

Currently, `low` = 0, `high` = 1.

Therefore, we choose as our guess index $guess = (0+1)//2 = 0$ and we compare `foot` with `bold`.

`foot` > `bold`. therefore we discard the upper half of the current range and the middle (or 'guess') element.

We do this by setting **`high`** = 0.

Now, we have `low` = 0 and `high` = 0. We have ended up with an empty range, therefore the query `bold` is not present in the original array.

Exercises in Sorting and Searching

5.7 Worked Example 7: Getting lucky on the first guess

We are given the (sorted) input array:

bike	bird	dorm	easy	lamp	park	unit	young
0	1	2	3	4	5	6	7	8

and we are trying to find whether `lamp` is present in the array.

We initialise two variables, `low` and `high` that denote the current range of indices where the query word may be located.

Initially, we set:

- `low` = 0

- `high` = 8

Step 1

Currently, `low` = 0, `high` = 8.

Therefore, we choose as our guess index $guess = (0+8)//2 = 4$ and we compare `lamp` with `lamp`.

Note that we have found `lamp` at index 4, and we are done.

5.8 Worked Example 8: Searching for a element not present in the input array

We are given the (sorted) input array:

bare	idea	oven	queen	view
0	1	2	3	4	5

and we are trying to find whether `pipe` is present in the array.

We initialise two variables, `low` and `high` that denote the current range of indices where the query word may be located.

Initially, we set:

- `low` = 0

- `high` = 5

Step 1

Currently, `low` = 0, `high` = 5.

Therefore, we choose as our guess index $guess = (0 + 5)//2 = 2$ and we compare `oven` with `pipe`.

`oven` < `pipe`: therefore we discard the lower half of the current range and middle element.

We update **`low` = 3**.

Now, we have `low` = 3 and `high` = 5.

Step 2

Currently, `low` = 3, `high` = 5.

Therefore, we choose as our guess index $guess = (3 + 5)//2 = 4$ and we compare `view` with `pipe`.

`view` > `pipe`. therefore we discard the upper half of the current range and the middle (or 'guess') element.

We do this by setting **`high` = 4**.

Now, we have `low` = 3 and `high` = 4.

Step 3

Currently, `low` = 3, `high` = 4.

Therefore, we choose as our guess index $guess = (3 + 4)//2 = 3$ and we compare `queen` with `pipe`.

Exercises in Sorting and Searching

queen > pipe. therefore we discard the upper half of the current range and the middle (or 'guess') element.

We do this by setting **high** = 3.

Now, we have low = 3 and high = 3. We have ended up with an empty range, therefore the query pipe is not present in the original array.

Printed in Great Britain
by Amazon